"Every Timothy needs a Paul. C. J. is mine…and this book contains his life-message. It is my handbook for pursuing a cross centered life. Read it yourself, and let God realign your life."

JOSHUA HARRIS
PASTOR AND BESTSELLING AUTHOR

"C. J. Mahaney is the most spiritually infectious Christian I know! His passionate pursuit of Christ is so enviable to me because it flows out of both his own daily contemplation of the Savior as well as his intimate knowledge of the Word of God. Would to God that all true believers be infected with a huge dose of the same kind of enthusiasm for living the cross centered life. If you read and seek to apply what C. J. skillfully writes in this wonderful book, you just might find yourself contracting the same glorious disease he has, with the joyful hope of spreading it all around!"

LANCE QUINN
PASTOR-TEACHER
THE BIBLE CHURCH OF LITTLE ROCK
LITTLE ROCK, ARKANSAS

"You're holding the book you want to read to begin living the Christian life. You're also holding the book you want to read to help you continue living the Christian life. There's no other place to begin living the Christian life than at the cross. There's no other place to keep living the Christian life than at the cross. C. J. Mahaney's *Living the Cross Centered Life* will help you do that."

MARK DEVER
SENIOR PASTOR
CAPITOL HILL BAPTIST CHURCH
WASHINGTON, D.C.
AUTHOR, *NINE MARKS OF A HEALTHY CHURCH*

"My friend C. J. Mahaney gives us a fresh look at our Lord and His cross. He lives the cross centered life, and is therefore qualified to talk about it. C. J. has a passion for Jesus and His people, and I was drawn closer to Jesus through this book. What higher complement could I offer?"

RANDY ALCORN
BESTSELLING AUTHOR OF *THE GRACE AND TRUTH PARADOX*
AND *THE TREASURE PRINCIPLE*

"C. J. Mahaney is one of our generation's most genuine and heartfelt proclaimers of the cross of Jesus Christ. In this unexaggerated book, readers will encounter the winsome zeal of a man who has found in Christ the greatest of treasures and a joy that must be shared."

DONALD S. WHITNEY
AUTHOR OF *SPIRITUAL DISCIPLINES FOR THE CHRISTIAN LIFE* AND
HOW CAN I BE SURE I'M A CHRISTIAN?

"The great nineteenth century Scottish pastor, Horatius Bonar once wrote, 'If we would be holy, we must get to the cross and dwell there.' C. J. Mahaney takes us to the cross in such a way that we can indeed dwell there. This is a book to be read and reread many times. Its message will never grow old or out of date."

JERRY BRIDGES
AUTHOR OF *THE PURSUIT OF HOLINESS*

"With tenderness and power, C. J. illustrates the critical difference between snacking on the benefits of the cross, versus surveying the wonders of the cross. It's the difference between living as consumers, versus loving as the consumed…the difference between having a theology of grace, versus running boldly to the throne of grace. This is a must and magisterial read!"

SCOTTY SMITH
SENIOR PASTOR
CHRIST COMMUNITY CHURCH
FRANKLIN, TENNESSEE

LIVING THE
CROSS
CENTERED
LIFE

C.J. MAHANEY

Multnomah Books

LIVING THE CROSS CENTERED LIFE
published by Multnomah Books
A division of Random House, Inc.

© 2006 by Sovereign Grace Ministries
International Standard Book Number: 978-1-59052-578-4

Portions of this book's content were previously published in *The Cross Centered Life* (© 2002 by
Sovereign Grace Ministries) and *Christ Our Mediator*
(© 2004 by Sovereign Grace Ministries).

Multnomah and its mountain colophon are registered trademarks of Random House Inc.

Printed in the United States of America

For information:
MULTNOMAH BOOKS
12265 ORACLE BOULEVARD, SUITE 200 • COLORADO SPRINGS, CO 80921

Library of Congress Cataloging-in-Publication Data
Mahaney, C. J.
Living the cross centered life / C.J. Mahaney.
p. cm.
ISBN 1-59052-578-7
1. Jesus Christ—Crucifixion. 2. Christian life. I. Title.
BT453.M32 2006
248.4—dc22

2005027558

08 09 10 11—10 9 8 7

To Nicole, Kristin, Janelle, and Chad.
May our Lord give you as much joy with your children
as you have given me.

CONTENTS

FOREWORD

by R. Albert Mohler, Jr., President
The Southern Baptist Theological Seminary

The book you now hold in your hands is nothing less than a manifesto for turning your world upside down. C. J. Mahaney wants you to know and experience the cross centered life. Thus, I need to warn you that reading this book will not be a safe and static experience. After all, the cross isn't about playing it safe; it's about being found safe in Christ—and that is the most exhilarating experience a human being can ever know.

In *Living the Cross Centered Life*, C. J. walks us through the real meaning of Christ's cross. He takes us right to the center of God's plan to save His own enemies—a rebellious humanity. As C. J. writes, "Because of God's amazingly gracious heart toward those who thoroughly deserve only His wrath, He both planned for and provided this mediator to resolve the divine dilemma—a mediator who, through His blood, would accomplish a unique assignment utterly unlike any other work of mediation. In the mystery of His mercy, God—the innocent, offended party—offers up to death His own Son, to satisfy His righteous wrath and save the guilty party from it."

That's about as clear a description of God's saving purpose as you will ever find. It is wonderfully grounded in Scripture (just read Romans 3:21–28!) and it points directly to God's mercy toward sinners. Of course, this takes us right to the cross of Christ and its meaning for us. He explains why the good news of the cross is so infinitely good, and how you can know the grace of God through the message of the cross.

I must also be honest with you. C. J. can be irritating at times. He tends to be very honest about sin and very clear about the fact that we can do nothing at all to deserve our salvation. This is a book that will humble the proud. Then again, that's the power of the cross. Our pride must be among the first things we surrender if we are to live the cross centered life. Like I said, this book isn't safe. The cross is deadly to pride.

C. J. also wants us to learn to celebrate the cross as the very ground of our salvation. "Move on to rejoicing in the Savior who came to save the worst of sinners," he urges. "Lay down the luggage of condemnation and kneel in worship at the feet of Him who bore your sins. Cry tears of amazement."

I can pretty much assure you that reading this book will be an emotional experience. After all, the cross of Christ is the very foundation of our salvation. What Christ did for us in dying on the cross must move believers to the deepest depths of emotion. At the same time, C.J. warns us against trusting our emotions as the barometer of our Christian experience. He teaches us how to live a mature Christian life that is centered in the cross and faithful to Christ.

Some books describe the objective reality of the cross without explaining how the cross transforms our daily lives. An even larger number of books commit the opposite error, trying to talk about the meaning of the cross while avoiding any biblical explanation of how God saves sinners through the cross of Christ.

C. J. Mahaney beautifully weaves these truths together and walks us into the transforming power of the cross. C. J. is a dear friend, and I can assure you that he lives what he writes. That's why he is such an influential Christian leader, and that's why you will find yourself connecting with his words.

Like I said, this book is a manifesto for turning your world upside down. May God greatly bless you as you read *Living the Cross Centered Life.*

AT THE CORE

*Life's Most Important Truth
Can Be the Easiest to Forget*

The Cross is the blazing fire at which the flame of
our love is kindled, but we have to get near enough for
its sparks to fall on us.

JOHN STOTT

Each of our lives is centered on something.

What's at the center of yours?

Think about it for a moment. What's really *the main thing*
in your life? Only one thing can truly be first in priority; so
what's at the top of your list, second to none?

Or let me put it this way: What are you most passionate
about? What do you love to talk about? What do you think
about most when your mind is free?

Or try this: What is it that *defines* you? Is it your career? A
relationship? Maybe it's your family, or your ministry. It could
be some cause or movement, or some political affiliation. Or

perhaps your main thing is a hobby or a talent you have, or even your house and possessions.

It could be one of any number of good things—but when it comes to centering our life, what really qualifies as the *one* thing God says should be the most important?

Maybe your life's passion is not so much a single focus as a constantly shifting gaze. After all, today's marketing culture bombards us with never-ending offers of something newer, something better. Sadly, an obsession with the latest innovation and the trendiest pursuit—and all in up-to-the-minute style— is as common inside the church as outside.

New things will always come along. Many will be useless, some will be good, a few will be better—but what's the one thing that's really *best*, according to God?

The Only Essential

Here's how Paul answers that question for us: "Now I would remind you, brothers, of the gospel I preached to you.... For I delivered to you as *of first importance* what I also received: that Christ died for our sins."[1]

First importance. Paul is pointing us to the one transcendent truth that should define our lives. In the midst of our various responsibilities and many possible areas of service in the kingdom of God, one overarching truth should motivate all our work and affect every part of who we are: *Christ died for our sins.*

This, Paul says, is the main thing. Nothing else—not even things that are biblical and honorable—are of equal or greater importance than this: *God sent His Son to the cross to bear His wrath for sinners like you and me.*

If there's anything in life we should be passionate about, it's the gospel. And I don't mean passionate only about sharing it with others; I mean passionate in thinking about the gospel, reflecting upon it, rejoicing in it, allowing it to color the way we look at the world and all of life.

The gospel is history's only essential message.

"The gospel," writes Jerry Bridges, "is not only the most important message in all of history; it is the *only* essential message in all of history. Yet we allow thousands of professing Christians to live their entire lives without clearly understanding it and experiencing the joy of living by it."[2] Neither you nor I want to be numbered among the believers who live out that tragedy.

That's why our attention must continually be drawn back to what John Stott calls "that great and most glorious of all subjects—the cross of Christ." In the Scriptures we discover a profound urgency for focusing all we are and everything we do around the gospel of the cross. For not only does this good news come first chronologically in our Christian experience, but it *stays* foremost in critical importance for creating and sustaining our joy and our fruitfulness—a fact we too often overlook.

OUR CONSTANT DANGER

A concern expressed by D. A. Carson, Bible scholar and professor at Trinity Evangelical Divinity School, is well justified: "I fear that the cross, without ever being disowned, is constantly in danger of being dismissed from the central place it must enjoy, by relatively peripheral insights that take on far too much weight. Whenever the periphery is in danger of displacing the center, we are not far removed from idolatry."[3]

John Stott agrees: "All around us we see Christians and churches relaxing their grasp on the gospel, fumbling it, and in danger of letting it drop from their hands altogether."[4]

Every day, we all face the temptation to move away from the gospel, to let it drop from our hands and hearts. Three main tendencies in particular tend to draw us away:

1. Subjectivism, which means basing our view of God on our changing feelings and emotions.

2. Legalism, which means basing our relationship with God on our own performance.

3. Condemnation, which means being more focused on our sin than on God's grace.

Later in this book we'll examine each of these tendencies more closely and discover how we can overcome them. But the first and most important thing you can do—*always*—is simply to make sure the gospel is at the very center of your life.

What's the main thing in your life? What is truly "of first importance" to you? It might be something perfectly honorable, perfectly legitimate; but if it's something other than the gospel—are you willing to repent to God and reorder your life?

Let me urge you to do whatever it takes to make the gospel your passion. Ask God to change your heart so you can personally affirm for your own life the words of Galatians 6:14—"Far be it from me to boast except in the cross of our Lord Jesus Christ."

WE NEVER MOVE ON

But maybe this thought is nagging you: If we as Christians have already come to believe in the gospel—if we've already received the gift of salvation He purchased for us with His precious blood—why focus any longer on the cross? Isn't it time to give our full attention to more "mature" matters of living out our faith?

Nope.

Read slowly and listen carefully to one of my favorite quotations: "We never move on from the cross, only into a more profound understanding of the cross."[5] The cross and its meaning aren't something we ever master.

In *Living the Cross Centered Life,* I hope to help lead you in that pursuit, in that pathway toward a more profound understanding.

George Orwell once noted that "sometimes the first duty of intelligent men is the restatement of the obvious."[6] One purpose of this book is to restate the obvious yet oft-neglected truth of the gospel of the cross of Jesus Christ and bring it before you again—vividly and compellingly—so that you more deeply grasp the crucial importance of never taking it for granted.

Do you think the truth of the cross is something you've already adequately understood?

If you think for a moment that the truth of the cross is something you've already adequately understood—if you suspect your life is already cross centered—allow me to bring to your attention some symptoms that arise from *not* being cross centered. Do any of the following describe you?

- You often lack joy.
- You're not consistently growing in spiritual maturity.
- Your love for God lacks passion.
- You're always looking for some new technique, some "new truth" or new experience to pull all the pieces of your faith together.

If you can relate to any of these symptoms, let me encourage you to keep reading. As you learn to live a cross centered life, you'll learn…

- how to break free from joy-robbing, legalistic thinking and living.
- how to leave behind the crippling effects of guilt and condemnation.
- how to stop basing your faith on your emotions and circumstances.
- how to grow in gratefulness, joy, and holiness.

These aren't the overhyped promises of an author wanting to convince you to read his book. These are God's promises to all who keep responding with their whole lives to the gospel of Jesus Christ and Him crucified.

Too many of us have moved on from that glorious plan. In our never-ending desire to move forward and make sure that everything we think, say, and do is relevant to modern living, too many of us have stopped concentrating on the wonders of Jesus crucified.

Too many of us have fumbled the most important truth of

the Bible, and therefore we've suffered the consequences.

But it's not too late to change. It's not too late to restate and reestablish the obvious truth as the *most important truth in your life*—and to be caught up as never before in wonder over the love and grace of God.

MORE REAL THAN EVER

In the church where I've served since 1977, our consistent pursuit has always been to keep the gospel central in everything we do. We never assume that there's already sufficient understanding, appreciation, and experience of "Jesus Christ and Him crucified."[7]

A while back I received a thank-you e-mail from a young woman who recalled her reaction when she first heard me identify the gospel as our church's lasting passion and priority. She told me, "I remember sitting there thinking...'What does he mean? Yes, we're saved because Jesus died for our sins. But don't we then focus on other aspects of the Christian life?'"

Meanwhile, under our teaching she began recognizing:

> that there was a problem deeper than my outward expressions of sin (harsh words, complaining, etc.)....
> I was learning about the sin in my heart and the motives at the root.... I vividly remember driving down the road one day, and God opening my eyes to see that I'm a wretched sinner to the very core of my being. In that second I thought, *What am I to do?!*
> Instantly I was clearly aware that this is why Jesus

Christ came and died on a cross—for me.... I laughed out loud, and said, 'My God, only You could show me what a wretched sinner I am and make it the greatest news I've ever heard!' The truth of Jesus' sacrifice became more real to me than ever before.

More real than ever before. Can you say that as well?

Luther once said he felt as if Jesus Christ died only yesterday. Is that how you feel?

Do you feel as if Jesus Christ died only yesterday?

Through what we experience together in this book's pages, I hope you'll learn to feel that way consistently, and become committed to live that way as well. As we cultivate our understanding and appreciation for the cross, as we live the rest of our earthly days feeling increasingly as if Jesus' death happened only yesterday, we'll be more and more astonished and overwhelmed by God's grace.

Only then will we more deeply understand and experience God's grace in a way that consistently engages our passion.

GRACE MORE AMAZING

I received another recent expression of thanks from a man who concluded his letter with these words: "I am amazed by the power of the gospel over and over, and have increased in my own love of the Savior. I can't believe that I have been saved from what I deserve."

Amazed by the power of the gospel, over and over—can you say those words about your own experience as well? Do you continue to find your salvation an incredible miracle as you recall the judgment you genuinely deserve?

If not…what can bring about a change? What is it that can make the gospel of God and His grace more deeply and consistently amazing to us? In our busy lives, how can we more often be gripped by gratitude and enflamed in passion for the Savior…and cast off lukewarmness and dullness in our spiritual experience?

For me, grace is never more amazing than when I'm looking intensely at the cross, and I believe the same will be true for every child of God. There's nothing more overpowering and captivating to the soul than to climb Calvary's mountain with childlike attentiveness and wonder, with all the distractions and wrong assumptions cleared away.

That's what we'll aim for in these pages. We'll trust our Shepherd to show us the unique path of righteousness He walked and to give us a profound glimpse into the depths of anguish it brought Him. It was an anguish infinitely darker than any death-shadowed valley you or I will ever pass through, but by better understanding His suffering, we'll grow in a consistent joy and zeal that will equip us for whatever trials God brings our way in the process of our sanctification.

Recalling John Stott's imagery in the quotation at the beginning of this chapter, we want to stay near enough to the "blazing fire" of the cross to be showered with its sparks and to find the flame of our love freshly kindled.

WORTHY OF AN ANGEL'S TONGUE

Before going on, I have to confess something personal: Although on most days I recognize how inept and inadequate I am in various areas, I'm never more acutely aware of my inadequacy than when I address the suffering of Christ and its meaning. I savor this privilege, yet when I teach and preach these things I consistently find myself physically weakened and emotionally overcome. So I acknowledge my dependence on God's strength in articulating this message, while also affirming my confidence in the One whose strength is made perfect in our weakness.

Our God is good, He is gracious, He is kind, and He's eager to glorify His Son and edify His people. So I proceed, full of faith in Him...and confident that by the Holy Spirit's prompting, you'll join me in tears and in unspeakably joyful gratitude as we climb up Calvary together and gain a deeper understanding of what really happened there, and the staggering reasons behind it.

The subject of the cross, Charles Spurgeon once said, "is worthy of an angel's tongue. And this also is true: It needs Christ himself completely to expound it."[8] In humble agreement with this prince of preachers on the infinite worth and wealth of this topic, I add as well the prayer it prompted from Spurgeon: that God would "by his own Spirit expound it to your heart."

CHAPTER ONE

THE CLIMAX AND THE KEY

Why the Cross Should Define Our Lives

The gospel cannot be preached and heard enough,
for it cannot be grasped well enough....
Moreover, our greatest task is to keep you faithful to this
article and to bequeath this treasure to you when we die.

MARTIN LUTHER

Imagine yourself at Timothy's side as he receives a letter from the apostle Paul—the letter that will be Paul's last.

You notice Timothy's hands slightly trembling as he breaks the seal and opens the parchment to read. He almost cradles the letter, as though his gentleness with it will somehow be conveyed to its author, now chained in a cold Roman dungeon.

These are written words that Timothy knows he'll return to often in order to carefully obey the apostle's guidance, but for now he reads quickly, hungering especially for personal news from his father in the faith.

A FINAL AFFIRMATION

Near the end of the letter, Timothy slows his pace. He can almost hear the encouraging voice of Paul:[9] "As for you, always be sober-minded, endure suffering, do the work of an evangelist, fulfill your ministry."

Then his eyes take in this line: "For I am already being poured out as a drink offering, and *the time of my departure has come.*"

For years Timothy has pushed aside the thought of losing Paul—this man who has been like a father, this friend and mentor who has guided and instructed the young leader. How could Timothy go on ministering without Paul's reassuring words, his confidence, his prayers?

Timothy stops reading to brush away his tears. How can he wallow in grief when his old friend faces death so boldly? "I have fought the good fight," Paul writes; "I have finished the race, I have kept the faith."

After staring up from the page for several moments, Timothy sits down to begin reading again from the beginning, slowly and deliberately. His eyes bore into each word, each sentence.

With Paul's life drawing to a close, what special insight has God given him to pass on? Timothy's heart pounds as the truth hits him with piercing clarity: There's no new secret revealed here, no previously hidden knowledge, but simply a stirring affirmation of the one truth Paul has lived for daily these past three decades, and soon will die for. It's the same truth for which Timothy, too, must spend himself: *the gospel of Jesus Christ and Him crucified.*

The words seem to shout from the letter:

Remember Jesus Christ, risen from the dead, the offspring of David, as preached in my gospel…

You don't need a new truth; you need to guard the one truth.

Timothy can almost see Paul's fiery eyes blazing into his own, can almost feel his gnarled fingers gripping his arm:

Follow the pattern of the sound words that you have heard from me, in the faith and love that are in Christ Jesus. By the Holy Spirit who dwells within us, guard the good deposit entrusted to you.

"You don't need a new truth," he hears his old friend saying. "But you do need to guard the *one* truth. Keep the *one* message."

HELD CAPTIVE

Paul simply refused to be pulled away from the gospel. The cross wasn't merely *one* of Paul's messages; it was *the* message. He taught about other things as well, but whatever he taught was always derived from, and related to, the foundational reality that *Jesus Christ died so that sinners would be reconciled to God.*

D. A. Carson writes of Paul, "He cannot long talk about Christian joy, or Christian ethics, or Christian fellowship, or the

Christian doctrine of God, or anything else, without finally tying it to the cross. Paul is gospel-centered; he is cross centered."[10]

John Piper agrees: "Paul was utterly mastered, held captive, by one great scene in history: a cross on Golgotha and on it the Son of God who loved us and gave himself for us."[11]

In every epistle, Paul kept the atoning death and resurrection of Jesus at the center—just as he did in his personal preaching and teaching: "I decided to know nothing among you except Jesus Christ and him crucified."[12]

Even Christ's resurrection was, for Paul, perpetually linked to the cross. Teacher and theologian Knox Chamblin explains:

His gospel is "the word of the cross" (1 Cor. 1:17–18); nowhere is there a comparable reference to "the word of the resurrection." In 1 Corinthians 1:23–24 it is "Christ crucified" who is identified as "the power of God and the wisdom of God," not, as might have [been] expected (especially in the case of "power"), Christ resurrected....

Both the cross and the resurrection of Christ are "of first importance" in Paul's gospel (1 Cor. 15:3–4). Unless Christ has risen from the dead, the preaching of the cross (and of the resurrection) is a waste of time (15:14); but once the resurrection has occurred, the cross remains central.[13]

For Paul, the gospel—this "word of the cross"—was no cold theological formula. Paul lived a cross centered life because the cross had saved and transformed his own life. Paul never forgot what he once had been, or the mercy and grace God showed him. This remained at the forefront of his mind. As he wrote on another occasion to Timothy, "Though formerly I was a blasphemer, persecutor, and insolent opponent.... *I received mercy...*and the grace of our Lord overflowed for me with the faith and love that are in Christ Jesus."[14]

MERCY THAT CAN'T BE FORGOTTEN

I can relate to Paul's amazement at being shown mercy and overflowing grace. I've lived in the same part of Maryland since I was a boy. Hardly a month goes by that I'm not reminded of who I once was.

Before God saved me from His righteous wrath in 1972, I, too, was a blasphemer. I lived for myself and my own pleasure. I lived in rebellion against God and mocked those who followed Him. I spent my high school and college years deeply immersed in the drug culture.

Sometimes, late at night, my friends and I would seek out quiet, isolated places where we could come down safely from drug highs. On more than a few occasions it was a D.C. monument. Other times a peaceful street under thick, deep trees. Or even the terminal at what was then a little-used airport called Dulles, where the doors stayed open long after the day's flights had ceased and we could move through the nearly deserted canyon of a building.

Someday soon I'll be near one of those places again, and the memories will flood back in. I'll remember what I once was…and be reminded of all I've received and experienced since then.

Often my eyes fill with tears at the memories of my foolishness and sin. And in the same instant, my heart will be filled with an unspeakable, holy joy. By the finished work of Jesus Christ on the cross, I've been forgiven of the countless sins I've committed.

This truth echoes far deeper than any drug can go.

"Blessed is the man," David wrote, "against whom the LORD counts no iniquity."[15] This truth echoes through my soul, resonating in places far deeper than any drug can go.

Many people today try to run from the past. I suppose I, too, could try that by leaving the hometown that holds so many reminders of my sinfulness. But I consider living here a gift from God. The regular reminders of my past are precious to me.

Why? Because, like Paul, I never want to forget the great mercy shown me.

A YOUNG MAN'S ESSENTIAL TRAINING

If you're a Christian, you don't need to live in the same place all your life to remember who you once were. And you don't need a background in drugs, or any dramatic conversion experience, for the cross to be dear to you.

Regardless of the differences in our backgrounds, we've all sinned and fallen short of God's glory.[16] My twelve-year-old son Chad's life is very different from how mine was at his age. He's being raised in a Christian home. He has been taught

God's Word. And unlike his father, he's surrounded by people in a local church who respect godliness and humility, not worldliness and pride.

But as Chad enters his teenage years and young adulthood, the most important thing I can teach him is that, even though he's being raised in a Christian family and is leading a moral life, he's a sinner who desperately needs the substitutionary death of Christ for God's forgiveness.

And so for years I've been teaching him the gospel, day by day. I tell him that he's a sinner just like his dad, and that sin is his most serious problem. I put it in words that his young mind can understand, but I don't ignore or minimize the seriousness of sin. Through his actions and attitudes he has rebelled against his Maker. And this great God is perfectly holy and must respond with fierce opposition to sin. He must punish it.

Some might find it surprising that I would teach a young boy about God's wrath toward sin. But I find it surprising that any loving person would withhold this truth from another person they love. Because only when we understand God's wrath toward sin can we realize that we need to be saved from it. Only when we hear the bad news that we're deserving of judgment can we appreciate the good news that God, through His Son, has provided salvation and full, continuing forgiveness for our sins. Only those who are aware of God's wrath are amazed at God's grace.

This is what I hold out to my young son as the hope of his life: that Jesus, God's perfect, righteous Son, died in his place for his sins. Jesus took all the punishment; Jesus received all the wrath as He hung on the cross, so people like Chad and his sinful daddy could be completely forgiven.

I hope to teach my son many other things as well, but the gospel is the one *essential* thing for him to know—as it is for us all.

The Climax and the Key

The cross climaxes the story line of the Bible—and it's the true climax of the story line of all our lives as well. The gospel's truth is to saturate our lives just as much as it saturates Paul's writings and all of Scripture.

The message Paul had for Timothy is the same message God has for you. You need to rediscover the truth. The key to joy, to growth, to passion isn't hiding from you. It's right before your eyes.

It's the *gospel*.

CHAPTER TWO

THE DIVINE ORDER

What You Feel vs. What Is Real

Oh, the havoc that is wrought, and the tragedy, the misery, and the wretchedness that are to be found in the world, simply because people do not know how to handle their own feelings!

D. MARTYN LLOYD-JONES

I grew up playing sports, and basketball in particular has always been a favorite. Though I turned fifty-one last year, I often remind my younger friends that I "still have game." I keep insisting that my quickness and three-point shot are as prime as ever—though they make it clear they don't entirely buy my self-assessment.

There's one thing, however, that I have to admit is particularly different from my younger days: I'm much more conscious of the importance of warming up before a game. I know from long experience that my muscles work best when they're prepared—stretched and warm instead of cold and tight.

We often need a warm-up just as much for our spiritual

and mental muscles, and I think that's especially true in this book. Before we push forward in the demanding spiritual exercise of more deeply experiencing the cross, we need to limber up our spiritual and mental faculties by exploring the whole matter of our *feelings*—to learn how they affect our view of reality and the way we live in response to reality. This is a critical conversation I need to have with you…and it can make all the difference in how much this book means to you.

If we want our hearts to be moved by the gospel, if we want our emotions engaged, if we want to be truly amazed…we have to start by putting our feelings in their proper place. So we need to slow down for a moment and contemplate God's order for truth-based living and thinking, an order which we have a tendency to disregard.

HOW DO YOU FEEL?

Have you ever considered how thoroughly most of us live by our feelings today—how feelings-focused we are? In a typical day, how often do you make decisions and evaluate reality based primarily on your emotions at the moment?

Take the process of reading this book, for example. My guess is that you've already encountered statements here and there that made you think, "How do I *feel* about this?" Perhaps without even being aware of this reaction, you were judging the merit of my words according to the subjective feelings you experienced while reflecting on them.

If so, you're not alone.

Our common tendency is to habitually begin with the

internal, the subjective, the experiential, then use those feelings and impressions to determine what we'll accept as being objective fact. We let our feelings tell us what's true, instead of letting the truth transform our feelings.

We let subjective impressions determine what we'll accept as objective fact.

For most of us, this isn't something we practice only while reading a book or hearing a sermon. We even explain our daily choices by saying, "I feel good about this," or, "I had a bad feeling about it." It's the fundamental mindset with which we approach practically everything. It's how we *live*.

We're conditioned to this approach not only by our sin but also by our culture, which incessantly entices us to "follow your heart" and do whatever makes us feel good—along with the flattering assurance that nonstop feeling good is something we absolutely deserve!

It would be fine to follow our feelings if we could always be sure they're faithful to reality. But they aren't; their perspective on reality typically has huge blind spots. As a result, our emotions are flighty, fickle, and far too easily dominated by any number of influences—spilled coffee at breakfast, a traffic stall when you're running late, a cutting comment from a coworker. Our feelings simply cannot be trusted.

SELDOM AMAZED

Even when it comes to our spiritual life, at any given moment we direct and locate our faith in our emotional state rather than in clearly objective truth. We tend to ask God for more "experience," then assure Him that if He'll give it, we'll acknowledge and believe His truth.

It happens frequently, for example, in our corporate worship. As people around us sing words expressing profound gratitude to Jesus for His death on our behalf, we may disqualify ourselves from truly entering into this adoration of our Savior because our "passion" is absent this morning.

It can happen also when we open our Bibles. Before us is a passage with words like *redemption, Savior, gospel, justified.* But if those words evoke little response in us, we unthinkingly pass over them to find something else that might light our fire. If the enthusiasm doesn't come quickly...well, we may just forget the whole thing. After all, who wants to spend the mental energy it takes to think carefully and intensely about the Scriptures? Who has time to study? Who has time to meditate?

> *In our arrogance, we invest our feelings with final authority.*

And this is how serious it gets: In our arrogance, we invest our feelings (or lack thereof) with final authority rather than recognize that our emotions tend to be unstable, unreliable, often governed by pride, and riddled with lies—lies that "feel" like the truth.

I've watched people yield to such lies repeatedly. It's a frightening experience to sit with individuals who actually insist that what they feel is ultimately more authoritative to them than what's written clearly in Scripture. They even somehow assume God is sympathetic to this attitude. But He is not. He would, in fact, identify it as the height of arrogance—which is something He's unalterably opposed to: "God opposes the proud," His Word declares.

That's the bad news. But in the same verse there's also good news: "God…gives grace to the humble."[17]

OUR FIRST RESPONSE

Who are these "humble" persons to whom God promises to extend grace?

The humble are those whose first response to objective truth from God's Word is not to ask, "How do I feel?" but to say, "I'm not going to let my faith be determined and directed by the subjective and the experiential. Instead I confess openly before God that I will believe the objective truth of His Word, regardless of how I feel."

D. Martyn Lloyd-Jones[18] once issued this warning: "Avoid the mistake of concentrating overmuch upon your feelings. Above all, avoid the terrible error of making them central." Anyone making this mistake, he adds, is "doomed to be unhappy," because of the failure to follow "the order that God himself has ordained."

And what is that order? Lloyd-Jones reminds us that "what we have in the Bible is Truth; it is not an emotional stimulus…and it is as we apprehend and submit ourselves to the truth that the feelings follow." When we focus first on truth, lo and behold, feelings follow! And they'll be *reliable* feelings, because they're anchored in truth.

That's the divine order.

Lloyd-Jones then proceeds to this profound application: "I must never ask myself in the first instance: What do I feel about this? The first question is, Do I believe it?"

GETTING THINGS IN ORDER

He's exactly right. It doesn't mean we *never* evaluate how we feel; that's just not where we're to start when we encounter truth. The starting place is choosing to believe the truth regardless of how we feel. Otherwise, we end up actually short-changing ourselves emotionally and experientially, since deep and profound feelings are the inevitable effect of Scripture rightly understood and believed.

As you read and meditate and think seriously about what's in your Bible, and believe and accept it, then ultimately *you will indeed experience it*, and *you'll feel the effect of it*. There's heart-transforming truth in the Scriptures, but you won't encounter it by first trying to feel it.

Most of your unhappiness in life is due to the fact that you are listening to yourself instead of talking to yourself.

Knowing and wholeheartedly believing the truth will always bring you, in time, to a trustworthy experience of the truth. But if you trust your feelings first and foremost, if you exalt your feelings, if you invest your feelings with final authority—they'll deposit you on the emotional roller coaster which so often characterizes our lives.

LISTENING TO OURSELVES

To exalt and rely on our feelings is what Lloyd-Jones called listening to ourselves instead of talking to ourselves. "Have you realized," he observed, "that most of your unhappiness in life is due to the fact that you are listening to yourself instead of talking to yourself?"[19]

I agree. Let me explain what Mr. Lloyd-Jones means by "listening to yourself." If you're anything like me, there's a good chance you do it every day. You know the routine. Every morning the alarm clock erupts, demanding attention.

Make it stop…make it stop! You hit the snooze button.

A precious eight minutes of floating, timeless oblivion pass. Then the grating alarm starts again. You open your eyes and the "listening" begins.

Today is…Thursday. Oh, no, sales meeting this morning! Yet another chance to see more incompetence in the company.

You roll over. But there's no more rest as you remember the weird noise the car started making yesterday…and the checkbook that needs balancing…and all the sarcasm expressed around the dinner table last night.

Life is just one big broken, whirring mess…

You slip out of bed. You know you should exercise, but your back is sore. *Forget it.*

As your bare feet hit the cold bathroom floor, the voice picks up its pace.

Can't anyone in this family learn to put the toothpaste back?

There's so much to do today, and you know you should pray.

But I haven't got time.

You didn't pray yesterday either.

No time.

You stare in the mirror.

Oh, I feel so drained…

The fleeting thought recurs that it might help to spend a few moments in prayer and reading the Scriptures.

But God feels so distant.

THE VOICE OF OUR FEELINGS

Can you relate?

On a daily basis we're faced with two simple choices. We can either *listen* to ourselves and our constantly changing feelings about our circumstances, or we can *talk* to ourselves about the unchanging truth of who God is and what He's accomplished for us at the cross through His Son Jesus.

I wish I could say I trusted God in that moment.

If you're anything like me, there's a good chance you do a lot of listening to yourself every day.

Not long ago, in the final stages of preparing my sermon to preach at church the next morning, I knocked a mug of hot coffee directly onto the keyboard of my laptop computer. The machine gasped out a mournful "fffttt!" and the screen went blank.

In an instant of clumsiness, I'd destroyed my computer, vaporized my sermon notes, and added hours to my preparation time. Frozen in disbelief, I stared dumbfounded at the empty screen. The keyboard took on the look of a small tropical swamp, its keys poking out of the steaming coffee like lily pads.

I wish I could say I trusted God in that moment. Nope. Instead I let out an angry, bloodcurdling *"Nooooooo!!"* Then I picked my chair a few inches up off the floor and slammed it back down.

Instantly I was convicted. God had been revealing a pattern of complaint in my heart and once again I'd sinned. Instead of trusting Him, instead of acknowledging that He was sovereign and I was just His servant, I'd yelled an angry, defiant "No!" to heaven and slammed my chair.

Almost immediately, the voice of my own feelings started to speak.

How could God allow this? Why is this happening?

Then this:

Oh, great—now you're sinning! You're a pastor? You're going to try and preach to others after that pitiful display of anger? How can you ask God to help you prepare now? This stinks. Look at what you've done!

I'm grateful that God helped me stop listening in that moment. I knew I needed to talk to myself. And because I knew I needed help, I went upstairs and involved my wife, Carolyn. First, she gently helped me see the sin that had caused my outburst. Then together, we reviewed the gospel.

Later, I went downstairs and began the tedious process of reassembling my message. But now I was talking to myself.

"Your sin of anger has been atoned for by Another. Jesus died for that sin. Jesus, the One who passed every test, who was tempted in every way but never sinned. He stood in your place and He was punished in your place. God has forgiven you and He's going to help you prepare and preach this message—not because you're sinless but because He is merciful!"

By God's grace I was able to turn away from what I felt and began to live in the goodness of what is true and unchanging—God's grace to me through the cross.

Thankfully, the sermon turned out fine. My computer didn't do so well, but that's another story!

OUTWARD INSTEAD OF INWARD

Another way to highlight this difference between talking to ourselves and listening to ourselves is to think of an outward, objective focus versus an inward, subjective focus.

As Scottish theologian Sinclair Ferguson notes, "The evangelical orientation is inward and subjective. We are far better at looking inward than we are at looking outward. Instead, we need to expend our energies admiring, exploring, expositing, and extolling Jesus Christ."[20]

We can learn to focus outward (and upward!), regardless of how we feel, because the gospel and its events remain completely unaffected by whatever is agitating our emotions. The gospel is objective fact.

That which is subjective changes regularly, like shifting sand. But that which is objective is built on solid rock. When we look inward, we live by the subjective, the temporal, the ever-changing, the unreliable, the likely-to-be-false. When we look out-ward, to the gospel, we live by the objective, the never-changing, that which is perfectly reliable and always completely true.

Our life in Christ is built on solid, objective truth. And of all the innumerable glorious truths of Scripture, the most criti-cal is that Jesus died for our sins.

EMOTIONS IN THEIR PROPER PLACE

The cross centered life starts with biblical thinking. Will you therefore build your life on what is real—or merely on what you feel?

Please don't misunderstand. I'm not advocating that we com-pletely ignore our feelings. Nor am I criticizing genuine spiritual experience, the kind of vibrant passion for God that Jonathan Edwards referred to as "religious affections." Quite the opposite! I'm in fact a passionate advocate of genuine spiritual experience and religious affections—*it's just not where we're meant to begin.*

"We think with our feelings," Ferguson has said.[21] It's true. We allow our feelings to guide our thinking, and we shouldn't. Emotions are a wonderful gift from God, and our relationship with God should bring strong godly affections to our lives.

We think with our feelings.

But our emotions shouldn't be vested with final authority. This should be reserved for God's Word alone.

Let me ask you: Where do you consistently direct your faith? What does it rest on? Is it your emotional state...or the objective realities that the Word of God and the Spirit of God have revealed? When you read or hear biblical truth proclaimed, what internal conversation takes place in your soul? Is your first reaction, *What do I feel about this?*

If so, do you plan to continue submitting everything ultimately to your feelings? Or will you instead trust in God's testimony, so that whenever you encounter biblical truth, your initial question will always be, *Do I believe it?* That's the only reliable way to transform your emotions…and to take them into a realm of love and adoration for the Lord that you've never before experienced.

WHERE IT MATTERS MOST

The divine order begins not with ourselves, but with God. And in this book we'll see how putting God and His objective truth first is never more applicable or valuable than when we draw near the cross, which is the hinge and center of human history. It presents an unfathomably stunning reality that we do well to return to again.

One Sunday morning, Charles Spurgeon was the guest preacher at a church in a country town in eastern England. Seated behind him was his grandfather, who was also a preacher. Spurgeon was speaking that day on Ephesians 2:8— "For by grace you have been saved through faith. And this is not your own doing; it is the gift of God."

As Spurgeon carefully explained this glorious gospel of grace, now and again he would hear the encouraging voice of his grandfather behind him, saying gently, "Good! *Good!*" At one point, he even heard this gentle prod from the old man's voice: "Tell them that again, Charles."

And of course, Spurgeon did indeed "tell them that again."[22]

Most likely you're no stranger to the gospel of grace and the basic truths of the cross of Christ. This book, however, is an opportunity for us to follow the wise exhortation of Spurgeon's grandfather and to see and hear these wonderful realities again, more clearly than ever, so that God's grace may astound us as never before.

CHAPTER THREE

SEARCHING THE MYSTERY

A Captivating Picture of His Love

Lest I forget Gethsemane,
Lest I forget Thine agony;
Lest I forget Thy love for me,
Lead me to Calvary

JENNIE EVELYN HUSSEY

The restaurant was uncrowded, and among the handful of early-evening diners were my wife and I on our date night. In the room's relative quietness, we could easily hear some of the conversation coming from the three parties seated not far away. At all three tables, the topic of extended discussion was Mel Gibson's film *The Passion of the Christ,* which had just been released. Hearing them talk, I felt a renewed sense of burden.

I'd first seen the movie myself only a few days earlier. Watching people enter the theater, many in a casual and fairly talkative mood with popcorn in hand, I sensed they were largely unprepared for what they were about to see. The mood of the audience changed quickly once the film began. I couldn't help noticing several people nearby in tears. And when it ended, there was mostly silence among the slowly dispersing crowd, with only a few hushed conversations. For a culture accustomed to thinking of the cross mostly as a piece of jewelry, seeing this movie was obviously a jolting experience.

Vast numbers of non-Christians watched *The Passion of the Christ* and witnessed its excruciatingly violent yet realistic images, and as a result, countless evangelistic opportunities opened up for our church and for Christians worldwide. For that, I'm profoundly grateful.

Images, however, cannot adequately convey the gospel's *content.* The gospel message isn't visual; it's truth. It is truth to be believed, not simply a collection of images to be viewed. Scripture is clear: "Faith comes from hearing, and hearing through the word of Christ."[23] It's only the *preaching* of the gospel, not the depiction of it, that God promises to accompany with saving effect.

Paul reminded the Galatians, "It was before your eyes that Jesus Christ was publicly portrayed as crucified."[24] These Galatians weren't present, of course, for the actual crucifixion of Christ; but it had been vividly and effectively portrayed to them *through Paul's preaching of the gospel.*

Although *The Passion of the Christ* brought millions to an unprecedented awareness of *how* Jesus died, it couldn't adequately convey *why* He died, and so the pronounced burden I felt was this: How could we as Christians explain to these moviegoers the true reasons behind Gethsemane and Calvary, as Paul did to the Galatians? Otherwise I feared that without a clarifying theological explanation, the movie's impact for most people would be only superficial, vague, and fleeting.

Do we adequately understand the deepest reasons behind the cross?

But do we ourselves adequately understand the deepest reasons behind the cross? If not, how can we take hold of those reasons—not only to be more compelled in sharing the good news of God's grace with others, but also to more fully and personally experience the gospel's "unsearchable riches"?[25]

ABIDING HARD BY THE CROSS

As we continue together in this journey, I'm attempting to follow the counsel of my historical hero, Charles Spurgeon, who wrote, "Abide hard by the cross and search the mystery of His wounds."[26]

Behind Christ's wounds are mysteries, mysteries that are revealed in Scripture. So we want to look carefully and study closely the purpose of our Savior's sufferings, from His agonized prayer in the garden to His cry of forsakenness on the cross. We want to look with more depth and detail at *why* He suffered and what He uniquely accomplished by His suffering in relation to God and for the sinner.

Throughout this book we want to let the Holy Spirit bring us "hard by" the cross—as near it as possible—and to "abide" there, staying and dwelling in its shadow. We want to unhurriedly observe the cross from sacred Scripture, pondering and reflecting on this event as we probe the mystery of Christ's wounds. We want to let the biblical writers take our hands and lead us where no movie can go.

What Does It All Mean?

Near the end of C. S. Lewis's *The Lion, the Witch and the Wardrobe,* the children Lucy and Susan are on the Hill of the Stone Table on a moonlit night. From a distance they watch tearfully as Aslan the lion submits to torment from the White Witch and her rabble of monsters—who are there because of the treachery of the girls' brother Edmund. He is bound, shorn of his golden mane, muzzled…then tied to the table and killed.

After these vile creatures have gone, the two sisters creep out of their hiding place to approach the table. They spend the rest of that night weeping over Aslan's body.

When dawn comes and the girls are shivering in the early morning coolness, they turn from the table to try and warm themselves by walking. As they watch the sky turn red and gold from the sunrise, they hear behind them "a great cracking, deafening noise."

They hurry back, and are overcome with yet more grief at what they see:

> The Stone Table was broken into two pieces by a great crack that ran down it from end to end; and there was no Aslan.

Suddenly their cries and questions are interrupted by "a great voice behind their backs."

They looked round. There, shining in the sunrise, larger than they had seen him before, shaking his mane (for it had apparently grown again) stood Aslan himself.

Susan tries to ask him if he's a ghost.

Aslan stooped his golden head and licked her forehead. The warmth of his breath and a rich sort of smell that seemed to hang about his hair came all over her.

"Do I look it?" he said.

Finally, after both girls have "flung themselves upon him and covered him with kisses," Susan asks a pressing question: *"But what does it all mean?"* [27]

A better question simply could not have been asked of Aslan—or, more importantly, of the Savior he so closely represents.

What is the meaning of the crucifixion of Jesus Christ? When *The Passion of the Christ* was released, a *Time* magazine cover asked, "Why did Jesus have to die?"—in other words, *what does it all mean?* No magazine cover ever asked a more significant or relevant question.

A BLOOD-STAINED PROPHECY

Surprisingly, one of the best places in Scripture to reflect deeply on the meaning of Christ's death is not in the New Testament, but in the Old—in a passage Spurgeon described as "the Bible in miniature and the gospel in essence." He was speaking of the fifty-third chapter of Isaiah.

This chapter "takes us to the heart of the human problem and the heart of the divine mind," according to Derek Tidball in *The Message of the Cross*; he calls it "one of the peaks of the Old Testament's revelation of God. From this vantage point we obtain a clear view of His work on the far-off summit of Calvary and gain a definitive perspective on its meaning."[28]

Isaiah 53 looks as if it were written beneath the cross.

Though Isaiah 53 was written some seven hundred years before Christ's death, "it looks," writes Franz Delitzsch, "as if it had been written beneath the cross upon Golgotha."[29]

No other portion of sacred Scripture gives us such a profound and detailed account of Christ's suffering on the cross—while revealing as well its glorious meaning. All of Scripture is blood-stained, but Christ's death is particularly pronounced in this passage. From his unique and inspired vantage point, the prophet Isaiah brings us right to the cross...so we can behold the Savior hanging there, and begin to understand what it all means.

THE APPEARANCE

In this profound chapter, God is speaking to His people about someone He simply calls "my servant"[30] (a designation referring unquestionably to the Lord Jesus Christ, as New Testament quotations of this passage make clear).

Isaiah portrays the Servant's origins in unimpressive terms:

"He grew up…like a young plant, and like a root out of dry ground."[31] In birth and background, the Servant appears to be nothing extraordinary.

Reading those words, we can almost hear New Testament voices: "Can anything good come out of Nazareth?" "Is not this the carpenter?"[32] The Messiah, when He came, was not recognized as royalty, nor was He from the religious establishment.

In physical appearance, the Servant is equally unimpressive: "He had no form or majesty that we should look at him," Isaiah writes, "and no beauty that we should desire him."[33] Rather than being strikingly handsome, he looked plain and ordinary—merely a typical Palestinian Jew. In fact, if somehow a group photograph could have been taken of Jesus and the twelve disciples, and we looked at that picture today, we most likely would be unable to distinguish which of those thirteen men was actually Jesus.

By all human standards this Servant fails to impress, and therefore, Isaiah says, "we esteemed him not." The Servant meets not only a lack of respect, but worse: "He was despised and rejected by men…and as one from whom men hide their faces he was despised."[34]

For just a moment, put yourself in the sandals of the original readers of Isaiah's prophecy. For twelve chapters—beginning with Isaiah 40—they have been reading about a glorious deliverance for their nation of Israel (following judgment and exile). For twelve chapters God has been giving them encouragement and comfort. Understandably they would expect this coming Deliverer to be a mighty warrior, a conqueror, someone like David.

Suddenly, in the context of this promised rescue, Isaiah is describing someone totally unattractive and unimposing—not someone acclaimed, but someone "despised and rejected"; not someone who conquers, but someone who is "crushed."[35] Reading this account for the first time, you would wonder: "Is *this* the guy who's supposed to deliver us? Can *this* guy even remotely be 'the arm of the LORD'[36] Isaiah promised?"

No wonder Isaiah begins chapter 53 with these words: "Who has believed what they heard from us?" Who has believed? No one. And that includes us, for apart from divine revelation and the Spirit's awakening, none of us would ever know genuine faith.

Human expectations of what a savior should be haven't changed much down through the ages. Seven centuries after Isaiah's prophecy, the apostle Paul would summarize people's continuing misconceptions: "For Jews demand signs and Greeks seek wisdom, but we preach Christ crucified, a stumbling block to Jews and folly to Gentiles."[37] By divine design the gospel is foolishness to all who through pride are governed by the wisdom of this world, restricted to human observation and impressed only by outward appearance.

THE REALITY

Isaiah then moves from human observation of the crucifixion to a divine revelation of what is taking place. In particular, verses 4–6 of Isaiah 53 plant us squarely beneath the cross.

These verses speak first of *our* condition—yours and mine. At least ten times in these lines we read the pronouns *our, we,* and *us*. But it isn't a pretty picture. It's about "our griefs," "our sorrows," "our transgressions," "our iniquities"; it's about how "we like sheep have gone astray; we have turned every one to his own way." That's *our* part in the divine drama unfolding here. We're mentioned only as contributing to the sin that makes the suffering necessary—and unimaginably excruciating.

We discover here as well that this totally unimpressive One, this suffering Servant, is suffering for us, and He's suffering as our substitute. That's *His* part in this divine drama— and He does it not at our request, and not with our encouragement and support, but while being despised and rejected.

> *This suffering Servant is suffering for us, as our substitute.*

The language of substitution—one person taking the place of another—pervades these verses, interwoven through the language of suffering. Isaiah tells us that the Servant bears our griefs, carries our sorrows, is wounded for our transgressions, crushed for our iniquities; "and the LORD has laid on him the iniquity of us all." Isaiah is showing us what the New Testament will later teach us in profound detail.

Earlier in this passage, Isaiah also shows us this about the Servant: "His appearance was so marred, beyond human semblance."[38] Because of the suffering the Servant endured for us, He became disfigured, deformed.

John Calvin wisely instructs us, "When we behold the disfigurement of the Son of God, when we find ourselves appalled by his marred appearance, we need to reckon afresh that it is upon ourselves we gaze, for he stood in our place."

"ALL DIE!"

In World War II, Ernest Gordon was a British captive in a Japanese prison camp by the River Kwai in Burma, where the POWs were forced to build a "railroad of death" for transporting Japanese troops to the battlefront. They were tortured, starved, and worked to the point of exhaustion. Nearly 16,000 died.

Gordon survived the horrors of that experience and wrote about it in a monumental work, *Through the Valley of the Kwai*, published in 1962 (and later made into the movie *To End All Wars*). He describes one occasion when, at the end of a workday, the tools were being counted before the prisoners returned to their quarters. A guard declared that a shovel was missing. He began to rant and rave, demanding to know which prisoner had stolen it.

Working himself into a paranoid fury, he ordered whoever was guilty to step forward and take his punishment.

No one did.

"All die!" the guard shrieked. *"All die!"* He cocked his rifle and aimed it at the prisoners.

At that moment, one man stepped forward. Standing at attention he calmly declared, "I did it."

The Japanese guard at once clubbed the prisoner to death.

As his friends carried away his lifeless body, the shovels in the tool shed were recounted—only to reveal that there was no missing shovel.[39]

Imagine, if you can, the effect upon his fellow prisoners of this man's substitutionary sacrifice for them. It's a profound and moving story of sacrifice and heroism. Yet it falls short of being an adequate illustration of the substitutionary sacrifice of Jesus Christ—because there *is* no adequate illustration.

Unlike the situation of those prisoners staring into the cocked and loaded gun of a deranged guard, you and I do not face death from a fellow sinner. What we face is the righteous threat of furious wrath from a holy God. *That* is the threat faced by all who have gone astray, by each one who has turned to his own way.[40] In our case, the shovel *is* missing; there is in fact a great deal more that's missing. We are indeed guilty of sin and deserving punishment.

But the innocent One, the holy One—God the Son—stepped forward to die for the rest of us. On that cross the Servant suffered *for* sinners like you and me, *because* of sinners like you and me—and as the *substitute* for sinners like you and me.

He takes the punishment that you and I richly deserve, yet in Isaiah's words we read, "We esteemed him stricken, *smitten by God,* and afflicted."[41] That was the word on the street—that's how the local media covered the crucifixion of Jesus of Nazareth: They said he was being justly judged by God for the sin of blasphemy.

Well, those who have been granted new eyes perceive that He was indeed smitten by God and afflicted—not for His sin, but for *ours.*

BE PERSUADED OF HIS LOVE

The motivation of God the Father in sacrificing His Son as our substitute is uniquely revealed—shockingly and startlingly exposed—in verse 10 of Isaiah 53: "It was the will of the LORD to crush him; he has put him to grief." The death of the Servant was not the fruit of human initiative and design; it was God's plan, God's purpose, God's *will.*

In the same month that *The Passion of the Christ* was released in movie theaters, *Newsweek* magazine filled its front cover with a close-up of actor Jim Caviezel as the bloodied and battered Christ, plus this blaring headline: "Who Really Killed Jesus?"

Isaiah gives us the answer.

Who killed Jesus?

God did. God the Father was ultimately responsible for the death of His Son. God is telling us, "I purposefully determined to crush My Son with My wrath—for *your* sins, as *your* substitute."

Why?

"Because I love you."

When you're tempted to doubt God's love for you, stand before the cross and look at the wounded, dying, disfigured Savior, and realize why He is there. I believe His Father would whisper to us, "Isn't that sufficient? I haven't spared My own Son; I deformed and disfigured and *crushed* Him—for *you.* What more could I do to persuade you that I love you?"

That's how far God's love goes.

And that is what it all means.

Listen to Sinclair Ferguson's words on the staggering implications of the crucifixion:

When we think of Christ's dying on the cross we are shown the lengths to which God's love goes in order to

win us back to Himself. We would almost think that
God loved us more than He loves His son. We cannot
measure His love by any other standard. He is saying
to us, "I love you this much."

The cross is the heart of the gospel; it makes the
gospel good news. Christ died for us; He has stood in
our place before God's judgment seat; He has borne
our sins. God has done something on the cross which
we could never do for ourselves. But God does something *to* us as well as *for* us through the cross. He
persuades us that He loves us.[42]

Are *you* persuaded?

If not…what *more* could God possibly do to persuade you?

If you recognize your need to become more overwhelmed
by God's love as revealed in the gospel, I implore you to keep
reading as we explore more deeply in the New Testament what
Isaiah has portrayed so starkly and surprisingly in the Old.

CHAPTER FOUR

THE DIVINE DILEMMA

*An Inescapable Penalty and
a Longed-for Salvation*

Men are opposed to God in their sin,
and God is opposed to men in his holiness.

J. I. PACKER

It was a crowded morning in Starbucks. I was standing with several customers who formed two parallel lines leading toward the counter. As my turn came to step forward and order coffee, the young man serving me smiled and said, "Hey, how are you?"

For a number of years I've been giving a particular response to that frequent question. I do it as a way of preaching the gospel to myself every day; I've also found it at times to be an effective opening for sharing the gospel with others. I used the words again that morning in Starbucks.

"Better than I deserve," I answered.

Immediately the guy behind the counter began challenging

my self-assessment. He was moved, I think, by compassion and a genuine concern that I was unreasonably deficient in my self-worth. When I didn't buy his assurances, he seemed irritated. Finally he challenged me, "Have you killed anybody?"

"No," I told him, "no, I haven't killed anybody." But I went on to talk about how serious my sin was. In that brief moment, I was able to introduce him to the doctrine of human sinfulness.

WORSE THAN LEPERS

Partway through the conversation, I turned to my right. The lady in the next line was staring at me, with a look as if to say, "I'd recommend decaf." In fact, the entire place seemed to be listening to my explanation.

I concluded by simply telling the young man, as I approached the point of tears, "I'm a sinner. And I need a Savior." And I meant it.

Considering how our sin must appear in God's sight, why are we still alive and breathing?

The conversation was ever so brief. When that moment was over, people around me seemed to gradually divorce themselves from what they'd heard and to return to whatever had earlier occupied their minds and hearts—still sadly unaware, I suspect, of how much they also needed a Savior. And unaware of what an unfathomable miracle it is that God allows their hearts to keep on beating.

R. C. Sproul wrote that the most perplexing theological

question is not why there's suffering in this world, but why God tolerates us in our sinfulness. Considering how our sin must appear in the pure sight of the righteous and holy God who created us, why are we even still here, alive and breathing? God's mercy is indeed an incredible mystery.

Luke tells us of the time while Jesus was "on the way to Jerusalem," and He encountered ten lepers. From a distance, they begged Him for mercy.[43] Knowing of their condition, we easily understand their desperate cry. Yet our own innate condition is far more serious than leprosy. In Starbucks I was surrounded that morning by lepers, fellow lepers who were born with a spiritual disease infinitely more subtle and sinister and abhorrent than any leprosy or cancer or virus ever known. Yet we rarely grasp the terrible threat facing each of us in our human condition, and so even less often experience astonishment over what God has done on our behalf to meet that threat.

The word *amazement* is related to the word *maze,* and its root meaning has to do with being perplexed and bewildered. But when you tell non-Christians, "God loves you," they aren't surprised, they aren't perplexed, they aren't stunned. Regrettably, the same is true among most evangelicals, who simply assume this gracious disposition of God—and therefore presume upon it. And we'll continue to do this until we learn to see our condition more fully from God's perspective.

The divine order requires starting with God rather than ourselves, and to start with God means gaining an understanding of our condition in His eyes as it stood *before* Christ's death.

For God, that condition involved a dilemma.

GOD'S INSOLENT OPPONENTS

Paul conveys this dilemma in the opening chapters of his first letter to Timothy. God is "the King of ages, immortal, invisible, the only God," Paul says.[44] As King of ages, He's the absolute Sovereign One who transcends time. In His immortality, He's immune to decay, to destruction, and to death. And He's invisible—living in unapproachable light, so that sinful beings cannot see Him and live. Furthermore, He's the *only* God, with no rivals.

In utter contrast to this is the portrait of humanity Paul paints for Timothy: "lawless and disobedient...ungodly and sinners...unholy and profane...those who strike their fathers and mothers...murderers, the sexually immoral, men who practice homosexuality, enslavers, liars, perjurers, and whatever else is contrary to sound doctrine."[45]

That's the biblical perspective on mankind—and all of us fit somewhere in that description.

Paul puts himself there as well, confessing that he'd been "a blasphemer, persecutor, and insolent opponent" of God.[46] Paul even identifies himself as "the foremost" of sinners, the worst sinner, the chief of sinners.[47]

God cannot simply overlook or excuse sin.

For God, the divine dilemma comes about because He isn't indifferent to any of this sinfulness on mankind's part. He is, in fact, righteously and furiously opposed to every bit of it. He cannot simply overlook or excuse it. In light of His holiness and justice, He has no alternative but to punish sin and punish the sinner. In our court systems, a judge who simply overlooked people's offenses and "just forgave" them would quickly be kicked off the bench. God is righteous, and must do what is right in punishing sin.

And yet, as Paul informs us, God "desires all people to be saved and to come to the knowledge of the truth."[48]

God's desire is to save—but how can He rescue anyone? He's righteously opposed to sin, yet sin lurks in every corner of every human heart. As we've seen, we're all "lawless and disobedient"; we're all "ungodly and sinners," as Paul says. Each of us to some degree can label ourselves the same way Paul did: an "insolent opponent" of God.

What an impossible predicament! A holy God can respond only in furious wrath to sin; how much more so when the sin is persistent, intrinsic evil! How could He ever forgive, pardon, save, and be reconciled with those who are entrenched and enslaved in such blatant hostility toward Him?

How?

IF ONLY

Tucked away in the book of Job is an agonizing glimpse of this dilemma from a human perspective—plus a hint of the solution God will provide.

In the midst of his suffering, the man Job is acutely aware of God's holiness, and he fears his afflictions may be an expression of God's judgment. Addressing these fears, Job at one point cries out, "How can a mortal be righteous before God?" After all, he knows that God "is not a man like me that I might answer him, that we might confront each other in court."[49]

Locked in hopelessness, Job somehow summons this desperate longing:

> If only there were someone to arbitrate between us,
>   to lay his hand upon us both,
> someone to remove God's rod from me,
>   so that his terror would frighten me no more.[50]

If only...if only there were someone to arbitrate between a suffering man and a holy God. Such an arbitrator, such a mediator, could indeed touch us both, lay his hand upon us both. Then somehow I could escape the terror of God's judgment. Job saw clearly the impassable gulf between humanity and God, yet somehow he could envision an intermediary to bridge that impossible distance.

In true reality, you and I have absolutely no hope...except to cry out for a mediator.

Can you put yourself in Job's place? In the true reality of the divine dilemma, that's exactly where you and I are in our humanity—ready to die under the righteous wrath of a holy Lord, with absolutely no hope...except to cry out for a mediator.

ANSWER TO THE CRY

We're quite familiar today in business and legal arenas with the process of mediation. Typically, two parties are in conflict, each feeling wronged or in imminent danger of being wronged by the other, but they share together a willingness to seek a solution through a neutral third party. This neutral mediator or arbitrator oversees the process of negotiation between the two parties, hoping for a measure of reconciliation and agreement that satisfies the perceived offense to both parties.

That picture's almost totally unlike the kind of mediation needed between God and humanity.

Both situations, it's true, involve parties in opposition. But in the conflict between God and man, only one party has been offended. God has been profoundly and acutely aggrieved by the other party; He Himself is fully innocent, entirely without fault or blame.

The other party (all of humanity) is undeniably, categorically, and completely guilty—yet this guilty party *doesn't even care to be reconciled*, but is locked in active hostility to the other party. In contrast, God is fully committed to resolution with the violators.

As we see this impasse more clearly…as we begin, by the convicting work of God's Spirit, to see and feel the weight of our own personal offense against God…we easily identify with Job's longing for a mediator who could "lay his hand upon us both."

The incredibly good news for all of us is that Job's desperate cry has been answered. There *is* someone to arbitrate between God and humanity. There *is* someone to touch us both.

CHAPTER FIVE

THE DIVINE RESCUE

Why Only Jesus Christ Could Save Us

The debt was so great, that while man alone owed it,
only God could pay it.

ANSELM

She was what psychologists call a "cutter"—and a friend of mine (who's a pastor) wrote me a letter in which he described an unforgettable counseling session with this troubled young woman.

It was her mother who had asked for the meeting, as my friend explained to me: "She related how her oldest daughter had been in the emergency room four times so far that year. Three times she had cut herself so deeply that stitches were required. Another time she had taken a bottle of pills, survived, and was detained in a psychiatric ward for teenagers. Now back at home, her daughter had cut herself again." The pastor agreed to meet with the daughter.

PROBLEM-SOLVING BLOOD

The next day, the woman's daughter walked into his office. My friend's letter explains how the session developed:

> She wore an oversized turtleneck with sleeves that went down almost completely over her hands. After a time of gentle questions and listening, the conversation turned to "cutting." She said that when she was upset with herself, or upset over the offenses of other people, she cut herself. It seemed to relieve the tension. Cleaning up from the bloody wounds distracted her from the other problems.
>
> She pulled up her sleeve and showed me her arm, and I don't think I will ever forget the sight. That image stayed in my mind for days and was painful every time I recalled it.
>
> What could I do? All I really knew about biblical counseling was to pray for people and to tell them about the gospel. Very small errors in a person's understanding of the gospel seemed to result in very big problems in that person's life.

The pastor pulled out a pad of paper and drew out for the young woman a diagram of the gospel. He agreed with her that blood can indeed "solve problems"—but pointed out that the blood "did not have to be her own, and that the cutting had already been done on her behalf. The Spirit brought illumination, and she prayed to accept the gospel."

At the time the pastor wrote this to me, six months had

passed since that meeting, and the young woman had gone the entire duration without cutting herself again.

Yes, it requires blood to solve our very worst possible problem. For God, who in His righteous wisdom determined that sin's just penalty is death, also determined that without the shedding of blood, there is no remission of sins.[51]

Our Mediator's work would be a labor of blood.

KEY TO THE BIBLE

If you were searching for a single sentence in Scripture to best capture the story line and theme of the entire Bible, what would you choose? Where would you look?

Many of us would no doubt go right to the beloved and familiar words of John 3:16, with good reason. But let me suggest we search no further than the place in Scripture we've already visited, the opening pages of Paul's first letter to Timothy.

Fix your thoughts on this sentence:

> For there is one God, and there is one mediator between God and men, the man Christ Jesus, who gave himself as a ransom for all, which is the testimony given at the proper time.[52]

J. I. Packer says it isn't too much to describe these verses as "the key, not merely to the New Testament, but to the whole Bible, for they crystallize into a phrase the sum and substance of its message."[53]

In this one sentence, Paul succinctly captures the main theme and essence of the entirety of holy Scripture—as well as answering the desperate cry we heard from Job for someone to arbitrate between God and man. Yes, Paul declares, there *is* a mediator! There's someone to arbitrate between us, to lay His hand on us both and remove the rod of God's wrath so His terror frightens us no more. There's a unique intermediary between God and humanity: the man Christ Jesus, who gave Himself as the ransom for all. The Bible's complete message hinges on this one point.

Because of God's amazingly gracious heart toward those who thoroughly deserve only His wrath, He both planned for and provided this mediator to resolve the divine dilemma—a mediator who, through His blood, would accomplish a unique assignment utterly unlike any other work of mediation. In the mystery of His mercy, God—the innocent, offended party—offers up His own Son to death, to satisfy His righteous wrath and save the guilty party from it.

"The glory of the gospel," says R. C. Sproul, "is this: The one from whom we need to be saved is the one who has saved us."[54] John Stott expressed it this way: "Divine love triumphed over divine wrath by divine self-sacrifice."[55]

UNIQUE MAN, UNIQUE WORK

But how could Jesus accomplish such an extraordinary work of mediation? An intermediary needs to represent both sides equally, yet in the conflict between God and humanity, the two sides are by nature as far apart as possible. How can

Jesus represent both in bringing them together?

Only someone both fully divine and truly human can effectively mediate between God and men, and Jesus is exactly that. He is unique—totally unlike anyone else. That's why Paul insists there's only "one mediator," just as surely as there's only "one God."

The work of mediation Jesus accomplished is likewise unique. Notice in Paul's statement how he transitions immediately from the Savior's birth—"the man Christ Jesus"—to His saving death—"who gave himself as a ransom for all." Christ's death was the purpose of His birth; Calvary was the reason for Bethlehem. God sent His Son to live a uniquely perfect life and die a unique death as the substitute for our sins.

Both Like Us and Unlike Us

Since sin has been committed by man, therefore sin must be atoned for by a man. Only a human being can be the perfect substitute for other human beings. The debt and obligation and responsibility are mankind's alone. Neither you nor I, however, can atone for our sin to satisfy God's righteous requirements; our own disobedience already condemns us before a righteous God. Furthermore, we're captive to sin; it's humanly impossible for us to release ourselves from its grip. Even if somehow, from this moment forward, we steeled ourselves to stop sinning (which is impossible), our record is still stained by the sins of our past.

That's our condition—having no possible way to atone for our sin, nor any possible way to free ourselves from enslavement to it.

A divine rescue is necessary. We need a savior! And in order to be our savior, in order to pay our debt, this individual must be *like us*—not just God in a form that merely appears to be human, but someone fully and truly human. Yet he must be *unlike us* as well, because he must be sinless, since only a perfect sacrifice is acceptable. He must be fully God, and not simply a man with a limited set of divine powers and abilities.

Author Ron Rhodes gives us helpful insight on this:

> If Christ the redeemer had been only God he could not have died, since God by his very nature cannot die. It was only as a man that Christ could represent humanity and die as a man.
>
> As God, however, Christ's death had infinite value sufficient to supply redemption for the sins of all mankind. Clearly then Christ had to be both God and man to secure man's salvation.[56]

No one else could do it. *Only Jesus Christ,* truly God and fully man, could be our substitute and make this sacrifice. Only Jesus could ever stand in this unique place and position. This One who lived the only perfect life also died a completely unique death as a ransom for our sin. He paid the price you and I owed to the innocent offended party, God our Creator and Judge.

Only Jesus Christ, truly God and fully man, could do it. No one else could.

Therefore the offended party is appeased. His righteous wrath against our sin is satisfied, having been poured out not upon us, but on Christ.

God's holy hostility against us has ended. The divine dilemma is resolved.

That's what Christ's death means to God.

No Better News

And what does Christ's death mean for us—for all who turn from their sins and trust in this unique mediator?

First, we have peace with God—the actual, objective reality of peace with Him, because His holy hostility against us has been spent against Christ instead.

Second, we no longer face condemnation from God when our life on this earth is over. Every believer in Christ can know that the moment we pass from this world and stand before God the righteous Judge, the verdict to be announced in our case will be "not guilty," by reason of the righteousness of Christ.

With full assurance we can anticipate and even experience that verdict *right now*. Our lives here and now are transformed as we live today in the joyful light of *that* day. We can live today free from the fear of wrath on that future date.

What amazing grace! There simply isn't greater news we could give to anyone, anywhere, at any time.

And you and I indeed have the privilege as well as the responsibility of proclaiming this good news. We've been entrusted with this unique message about this unique Mediator, and we're the sole guardians of it. That's why we must deeply understand it ourselves and take it to heart, so we can share it accurately and passionately with others.

And now, having brought these incredible realities of Christ's mediation into clearer focus, we can proceed to Gethsemane and ultimately draw near the cross to more deeply understand our Savior's suffering…and to be more affected by it.

CHAPTER SIX

STARING INTO THE CUP

The Shock of Gethsemane

The garden of Gethsemane is one of the most sacred
and solemn scenes in the entire Bible.

SINCLAIR FERGUSON

Gethsemane is a moment that floors us. A change so abrupt, so
pronounced, that it shocks our very soul.

When we look at Jesus in the pages of the unfolding
Gospels—allowing ourselves to walk closely alongside Him
through those three exciting years of ministry—words like
authoritative, assured, and *fearless* truly describe Him. He's
unfailingly steady and controlled.

But there comes a moment, as we follow Him into "a place
called Gethsemane,"[57] when all is radically changed. Suddenly
we encounter a Savior we're unfamiliar with. What we observe
is foreign and frightening.

Jesus "began to be greatly distressed and troubled," Mark's

Gospel tells us.[58] "He began to be gripped by a shuddering terror and to be in anguish," one translation renders it. Other versions use the words *horror, deep alarm, dismay.*

This is a consuming, crushing agony for our Savior, utterly unlike anything we've previously observed.

NEARLY DYING

Remember those days in Galilee? We saw His extended hand offering one tender touch after another as He healed sickness and forgave sin. We saw His strong arms outstretched with power as He cast out demons and raised the dead. We saw Him striding serenely on the surface of a wave-tossed sea on a stormy night. We saw Him seated tranquilly in a little fishing boat in shallow, sun-sparkled water beside a shoreline packed with listening crowds astounded and delighted by His incomparable teaching.

On a grassy hillside, we saw genuine gratitude on His upraised face as He gazed into the heavens and blessed a few loaves and fishes; we caught His smile of compassion as He handed out the fragments to feed thousands. In awe we watched Him on a rocky, cloud-wrapped summit as His face and form were wondrously transfigured in supernatural light.

Then here in Jerusalem, in the crowded temple courts, our eyes were wide in amazement as He stood up to the religious establishment and confronted their hypocrisy without the slightest qualm of intimidation, even to the point of fashioning a whip and chasing out their moneychangers.

Consistently He has been bold, He has been brave, He has been calm.

It's true we've also seen Him tearful and disquieted; when He came to Bethany after His friend Lazarus died, He was deeply troubled, and at the tomb He openly wept. But that was far different from the sheer torment we see overtaking Him now, under these twisting, moonlit branches of Gethsemane's olive grove.

The sorrow in this moment is so pronounced that He actually draws near to dying.

Jesus turns to Peter and James and John and tells them, "My soul is very sorrowful, even to death." *Even to death!* This is no hype; He means it. The sorrow in our Savior's soul at this moment is so powerful and pronounced that He actually draws near to dying in His human experience—even now, several hours before the coming torture of the cross.

After urging these three disciples to be watchful, Jesus steps a short distance beyond…and staggers to the stony ground.[59] So horrific is the burden upon Him that He cannot even remain in an upright position.

UNPREPARED

We're seeing Jesus more vulnerable and more human than we've ever known. And we can't escape one question:

Why?

Why this shuddering terror, this staggering distress?

Even this very night there was no prior indication of such anguish. Earlier this evening, with solemn dignity, He inaugurated the Lord's Supper with His disciples and led them in singing a hymn. It's true that in the upper room He "was troubled in his spirit"[60] as He foretold His betrayal, and that He informed the disciples they would "all fall away"—yet in almost the same breath He confidently reminded them, "But after I have risen, I will go ahead of you into Galilee."[61]

It's not as if Jesus is surprised by death's approach. He long ago determined to bear God's judgment for sin as our substitute, and for months He has discussed His death repeatedly with His disciples.

Nor is He avoiding or postponing the hour of sacrifice for which He came to this earth. Quite the opposite. When it was no secret to anyone that Jerusalem was a hotbed of hostility against Him, He was out in front of His disciples, leading them toward the city without a trace of reluctance—so that "they were amazed, and those who followed were afraid."[62] The fear and anxiety belonged to His followers, not to Jesus.

So nothing has prepared us for Gethsemane, for this abrupt horror, this deep distress.

And we wonder: *Why?*

What It Meant to Him

Here's why: In this garden, our Savior is beginning to confront as never before the ultimate and deepest agony of Calvary—an agony that will go infinitely beyond any *physical* aspects of His suffering.

For Jesus, the cross will bring incomparable and unprecedented suffering of wrath and abandonment. His downward path into those unspeakable depths begins to plunge steeply in this garden called Gethsemane.

And as we follow into the garden to observe Him, we have to realize that what transpires here is so far beyond our depth, so far beyond our ability to comprehend. I find a verse from an old hymn particularly relevant:

> Oh help me understand it,
>   help me to take it in—
> what it meant to Thee, the Holy One,
>   to bear away my sin.[63]

We need divine assistance to "take it in," to absorb deeply what bearing away our sin meant to Jesus, the holy One. That's what we're after—what it meant *to Him*.

THE DETESTABLE DRINK

Step closer with me under the shadow of the trees…let's watch and listen.

As Jesus lies prostrate on the ground, we overhear Him praying: "Abba, Father, all things are possible for you. Remove this cup from me. Yet not what I will, but what you will."[64]

He's making this plea repeatedly. With His face to the ground, we can see sweat on His temples. He lifts His head, and His expression reveals an agony so intense that His sweat is "like great drops of blood falling down to the ground."[65]

His words tell us why: "Remove this *cup*," Jesus pleads again. In this moment, there's no doubt what is dominating His heart and mind.

What is this cup? It's clearly a reference to the wrath of God for your sins and mine.

If we knew the Scriptures as Jesus does—Scriptures that no doubt have been much on His mind in these hours—we couldn't escape this reference. Isaiah 51:17 shows us this cup in God's extended hand—it's "the cup of his wrath," and for those who drink from it, it's "the cup of staggering." This cup contains the full vehemence and fierceness of God's holy wrath poured out against all sin, and we discover in Scripture that it's intended for all of sinful humanity to drink. It's your cup…and mine.

In the vivid imagery of the Old Testament, this cup is filled with "fire and sulfur and a scorching wind"[66] like some volcanic firestorm, like all the fury of the Mount St. Helens eruption concentrated within a coffee mug. No wonder Scripture says that tasting from this cup causes the drinker to "stagger and be crazed."[67] No wonder that when Jesus stares into this detestable vessel, He stumbles to the ground.

That's why there's shuddering terror and deep distress for Him at this moment. In the crucible of human weakness He's brought face-to-face with the abhorrent reality of bearing our iniquity and becoming the object of God's full and furious wrath.

HELL, NOT HEAVEN

What Jesus recoils from here is not an anticipation of the physical pain associated with crucifixion. Rather it's a pain infinitely greater—the agony of being abandoned by His Father.

As one Bible commentator notes, Jesus entered the garden "to be with the Father for an interlude before his betrayal, but found Hell rather than Heaven open before him."[68] Knowing the hour for His death is fast approaching, Jesus has come here in need as never before of His Father's comfort and strength. Instead, hell—utter separation from God—is thrust in His face.

We hear Him cry out: Father—is there an alternative? Is there any way to avoid this? If there's a way this cup could pass from Me, *would You please provide that to Me?*

Silence. We can see it in His face—Jesus receives no answer to this desperate entreaty.

A second time He pleads for an alternative to that horror of abandonment by His Father. If such an alternative existed, the Father would most surely provide it. But the obedient Son's plea to His loving Father is met with silence. *Why?*

Listen to this verse again for the very first time: *For God so loved the world…*that He is silent to His Son's agonizing appeal.

This is what bearing our sin means to *Him*—utter distress of soul as He confronts total abandonment and absolute wrath from His Father on the cross, a distress and an abandonment and a rejection we cannot begin to grasp.

In this, our Savior's darkest hour…do you recognize His love for you?

ANOTHER CUP

Listen again to the precious and powerful words we hear Him repeat to His Father:

"Yet not what I will, but what You will."

"Yet not what I will, but what You will."

"Yet not what I will, but what You will."

Jesus is saying, "Father, I willingly drink this cup by Your command—I'll drink it all."

And He will. He'll drink all of it, leaving not a drop.

Not only will He leave nothing in that cup of wrath for us to drink…but today you and I find ourselves with another cup in our hands. It's the cup of salvation. From this precious new cup we find ourselves drinking and drinking—drinking consistently, drinking endlessly, drinking eternally…for the cup of salvation is always full and overflowing.

We can drink from this cup only because Jesus spoke those words about the other cup: "Yet not what I will, but what you will."

I will drink it all.

As we watch Jesus pray in agony in Gethsemane, He has every right to turn His tearful eyes toward you and me and shout, "This is *your* cup. *You're* responsible for this. It's *your* sin! *You* drink it." This cup should rightfully be thrust into my hand and yours.

Instead, Jesus freely takes it Himself…so that from the cross He can look down at you and me, whisper our names, and say, "I drain this cup for you—for you who have lived in defiance of Me, who have hated Me, who have opposed Me. I drink it all…for *you*."

This is what our sin makes necessary. This is what's required by your pride and my pride, by your selfishness and my selfishness, by your disobedience and my disobedience. Behold Him…behold His suffering…and recognize His love.

CHAPTER SEVEN

YOUR FACE IN THE CROWD

Our Part in the Savior's Death

We may try to wash our hands of responsibility like Pilate,

but our attempt will be futile, as futile as his.

For there is blood on our hands.

JOHN R. W. STOTT

We saw Jesus enter Gethsemane shuddering, His soul deeply distressed.

But when He emerges from the garden, He's no longer trembling and troubled. Instead we see Him composed and authoritative as He tells the disciples, "Are you still sleeping and taking your rest? It is enough; the hour has come. The Son of Man is betrayed into the hands of sinners. Rise, let us be going; see, my betrayer is at hand."[69]

What explains this transformation? Only His obedience.

STRENGTH TO ENDURE

Though there was silence in answer to the Son's request for an alternative to the cross, the Father hasn't withheld comfort and strength to His obedient Son. In fact, at the close of Christ's prayer in Gethsemane, "there appeared to him an angel from heaven, strengthening him."[70] That provision of strength will continue to sustain Jesus in the hours of trial and torture that quickly unfold.

An armed force, led here by Judas, comes to arrest Jesus, and we follow as the soldiers take Him away. His disciples flee into the night.

A few hours later we see the continued inner strength of Jesus as He stands before Pilate. He stays remarkably silent in the face of accusations from the chief priests and elders, so that Pilate asks, "Do you not hear how many things they testify against you?" Still Jesus gives no answer, so that the governor is "greatly amazed."[71]

Why does Jesus have no reply to these bogus charges?

Have you ever wondered, as I have, why Jesus has no reply to these bogus charges? It seems that He could easily persuade Pilate, who shows respect for Jesus and who certainly has no affection for the chief priests and elders; he knows what they're about.

But Jesus knows this is the hour for which He was born. This is the reason He's come into the world, and He in no way wants to resist it. He was born to die as our mediator. You and I know we're going to die; what we don't know is when or how. But Jesus knew when, He knew how...and most importantly, He knew why.

As John Stott says, what dominated Jesus' mind wasn't so much the living of His life but the *giving* of it. This indeed was the Savior's own testimony: "The Son of Man came…to give his life as a ransom for many."[72] So He offers His accusers no rebuttal or protest, and Pilate is astounded.

IRRESISTIBLE FORCE

The governor then tries to help Jesus by taking advantage of a Passover custom in which authorities free one prisoner whom the public most wants to see released. Pilate offers the gathered crowd a choice between Jesus and a "notorious prisoner"—a terrorist named Barabbas.[73]

Meanwhile Pilate, seated on the judgment seat, receives an extraordinary message from his wife. We look over his shoulder as he reads it. Her note mentions that she "suffered much" in a dream about Jesus; therefore she counsels her husband, "Have nothing to do with that righteous man."[74] Here is conspicuous support for the innocence of Jesus—and further incentive for Pilate to let Him go.

While the governor reflects on his wife's appeal, we make our way to the gathered crowd and see the chief priests and the elders circulating skittishly among the people. They're urging everyone "to ask for Barabbas and destroy Jesus."[75]

Pilate puts away his wife's note. He stands and asks the throng, "Which of the two do you want me to release for you?"

All around us, the mob is fully incited. They quickly cry, "Barabbas."

"Then what shall I do with Jesus who is called Christ?"

The response—from "all" of them, we read—is this: "Let him be crucified!"

"Why, what evil has he done?" the governor asks.

Everywhere around us, the mob shouts all the more: "Let him be crucified!"[76]

Luke emphasizes that the throng was "urgent," "demanding," and "loud," and that "their voices prevailed."[77] Here's a force that Pilate can neither suppress nor ignore.

THERE THAT DAY

Let me ask you: With whom do you most identify in the events of this dark day? Of the many onlookers and participants in these scenes, whose actions are most like your own, if somehow you were also there?

For some it might be Peter, weeping bitterly in the predawn hours as the weight of his denial of the Lord bore down upon him.

For others it might in some way be the passerby Simon of Cyrene, who was forced to carry Jesus' cross for Him. Others would identify with the women who were followers of Jesus and who "stood at a distance watching these things."[78]

Some would perhaps choose Mary, His mother, who was "standing by the cross of Jesus," enduring such unimaginable pain.[79] Or the disciple John, who also was "standing nearby" and whom Jesus spoke to from the cross.[80] Or the penitent thief, who from his own cross cried out to the Savior in faith, "Jesus, remember me when you come into your kingdom."[81] Or the centurion who, after watching how Jesus died, was moved to say, "Truly this man was the Son of God!"[82]

But let me tell you who I identify with.

I identify most with the angry mob screaming, *"Crucify Him!"*

That's who we should all identify with. Because apart from God's grace, this is where we would all be standing, and we're only flattering ourselves to think otherwise. Unless you see yourself standing *In the events of this dark day, with whom do you most identify?* there with the shrieking crowd, full of hostility and hatred for the holy and innocent Lamb of God, you don't really understand the nature and depth of your sin or the necessity of the cross.

FROM OUR HAND

As those shouts and screams from the mob grow in volume, what's it like for our Lord to look out upon these people? Even if you can't recognize yourself among the angry faces, or distinguish your own strident voice…*He* can. And in response to those sinful shouts and curses from you and me, Jesus yields to the sentence of death.

A great hymn from the pen of the Scottish pastor Horatius Bonar helps us realize our responsibility in the Savior's death sentence. It includes these lines:

'Twas I that shed that sacred Blood,
    I nailed him to the Tree,
I crucified the Christ of God,
    I joined the mockery.[83]

When we begin to grasp that *we* joined that mockery—that *we* are to blame for the Savior's death—we start to understand the seriousness of our sin.

But convicting you of sin is not my ultimate purpose here; rather, I want to convince you of grace. For when you're deeply aware of your sin, and of what an affront it is to God's holiness, and of how impossible it is for Him to respond to this sin with anything other than furious wrath—you can only be overwhelmed with how amazing grace is.

Only those who are truly aware of their sin can truly cherish grace.

CHAPTER EIGHT

THE SCREAM OF THE DAMNED

Our Savior's Worst Torment

This cry represents the most agonizing protest
ever uttered on this planet.
It burst forth in a moment of unparalleled pain.
It is the scream of the damned—for us.

R. C. SPROUL

As the terrible events of this day continue to unfold, our sinful humanity is shown at its worst. The soldiers spit on Him and strike Him on the head. They strip Jesus, drape a scarlet robe on His shoulders, push a crown of twisted thorns on His head, and place a reed in His right hand. Kneeling before Him, they mock Him: "Hail, King of the Jews!"[84]

Ironically, their mocking words are in fact revealing truth. Their victim is not only King of the Jews, but God's appointed King over all creation, and one day every knee will bow before Him, including the knees of these soldiers who torture Him.

PROPHETIC MOCKERY

You and I follow along as the Romans lead Jesus away to the hill called Golgotha—"Place of a Skull." They nail His quivering flesh onto a cross, then raise it and slam it into the ground.

From all around us in the throng of onlookers, the verbal abuse continues. Those passing by wag their heads and say, "If you are the Son of God, come down from the cross." The chief priests and the scribes and the elders echo the mockery: "He saved others; he cannot save himself."[85]

Make no mistake: Jesus can descend from the cross and save Himself at any moment. It isn't the nails that keep Him there. What keeps Him there is what placed Him there—His passion to do the will of His Father, and His love for sinners like you and me.

Without their knowing it, the mocking words these onlookers utter do in fact reveal the uniqueness of the Savior's death and why it mattered. In their spiritual blindness they in effect express sublime spiritual truth. For Jesus cannot both save Himself and save you and me. It's precisely because He refused to save Himself that He's able to save others.

It isn't the nails that kept Him on the cross.

It would be necessary for Him to die even if it were for your sin alone or my sin alone. That's why you and I are fully responsible for this tragic death. As John Stott wisely observed, "Until you see the cross as that which is done *by* you, you will never appreciate that it is done *for* you."[86]

Luther said that we all carry in our pocket His very nails. Are you aware of those nails in your possession?

CRUSHING DARKNESS

For hours we see Him hanging suspended between heaven and earth in a pain we can't imagine—and yet without complaint, without protest. Instead, we hear this: "Father, forgive them, for they know not what they do."[87]

Meanwhile, at midday, a darkness comes over the land—not from an eclipse or overcast skies, but a supernatural darkness, an atmospheric confirmation of the judgment of God. Can you imagine such a gloom? It's a darkness you can feel.

Even the sky reflects what is happening to the Son of God. Jesus is being made to drink from that cup which He had asked at Gethsemane to be removed. He's being made to experience the full fury of the wrath of God—the intense, righteous hatred of God for sin, a wrath that has been stored up beginning with Adam's sin and extending to all of your sin and mine, and to all the sin to the end of this world's history.

The sinless One—innocent and holy Himself—is made the object of that vast and vile immensity of sin. This is His severest test, His cruelest and most demanding ordeal, a torment far beyond the pain of His physical suffering.

ABLE TO BEAR IT NO LONGER

In this strange, unnatural darkness, by the flickering light of the soldiers' torches, we step closer to the cross to watch and listen.

Suddenly His face contorts in a display of anguish more terrible than anything we've yet seen. He can restrain Himself no longer. He screams out, "My God, my God!"

Why
have You
forsaken
me?

"Nowhere in all the Bible," writes one author, "do we encounter any mystery that so staggers the mind and shocks the Christian consciousness as this tortured cry from the lips of our dying Savior."[88]

The cry is a question—but Jesus is not accusing His Father; nor is He perplexed as to why He's dying. It's a question from David's words in Psalm 22, and on the cross our Lord is fulfilling that messianic psalm. But Jesus is also doing more than that. He's experiencing on the cross what no one in human history ever has or ever will experience. He's receiving what you and I should be receiving—His Father's full and furious wrath. He's experiencing what every other human being in history deserves and what He alone does *not* deserve.

And He's experiencing it *alone.* Have you ever felt truly alone?

TRUE ALONENESS

After my father died, I gathered with our family at a funeral home to choose the casket and arrange specifics for the memorial service. As I drove away from the funeral home, I made it only about two hundred yards before I broke down and wept, and had to pull the car over and stop.

This wasn't the first time I'd cried after my father's death, but it was the first time I'd cried *alone,* and the tears and the grief were so strong. Cars streamed past me, their passengers and drivers unaware of what was taking place in my car, and I vividly remember how alone I felt.

But in truth I wasn't alone, because only two hundred yards away were people who loved me with all their hearts. To be comforted, all I needed to do was turn around and go back to the funeral home. I felt alone—but I really wasn't.

For me, personally, the sense of aloneness in that moment was overwhelming; yet I know that many others have experienced a depth of loneliness or even abandonment and rejection far worse than anything I went through. Many have wept as I did, but could never be assured there was someone nearby they could turn to for comfort, whether two hundred yards away or two hundred miles.

And yet, even in comparison to such unbearable experiences, there's Someone else whose pain of isolation and abandonment goes infinitely deeper.

Before being nailed to the cross, Jesus already knew what it meant to be forsaken; He had become intimately acquainted with being rejected or abandoned by men. Yet whenever it happened, He could always say, "Though forsaken by men, I am not alone, for My Father is always with Me."

In the Father's sight, the monstrous totality of human sin is resting upon one Man.

But not now.

He who for all eternity has never been alone is now wholly abandoned. Such utter desolation has never even existed before in all eternity, because of the infinite love and fellowship of the Trinity, which can never be broken. But now the incarnate Son must be forsaken by the Father…because the Father is holy, and there in the Father's sight is "the most grotesque display of ugliness imaginable," as R. C. Sproul termed it.[89] It's the monstrous sight of the unbounded totality of human sin resting upon one Man.

Therefore that Man must be utterly removed from the presence of the holy God, utterly separated, as far as the east is from the west.

Jesus doesn't just *feel* forsaken; He *is* forsaken. In an unfathomable mystery, at that moment, as God's wrath is poured upon Him as the substitute for our sin, Jesus is rejected by God. His Father turns away from Him. It isn't a deceptive feeling; it's *reality.*

In Gethsemane, when Jesus looked into the cup, this is what He had seen. This is what had staggered Him.

THE MIRACLE

What could possibly be more amazing? And what greater reason can there be for you and me at this very moment to praise and thank Him?

The personal desolation Christ is experiencing on the cross is what you and I should be experiencing—but instead, Jesus is bearing it, and bearing it all alone.

Why alone?

He's alone so that we might never be alone.

He cries out to God, "Why have You forsaken Me?" so that you and I will never have to make a similar cry. He was cut off from His Father so that we can boldly say, "Nothing shall separate us from the love of God in Christ Jesus."

He's forsaken so that we might be forgiven.

Please don't ever grow overfamiliar with forgiveness. What a miracle it is! What a gift from God! Our forgiveness is a fact that not only was accomplished through Christ's rejection and abandonment on the cross, but was confirmed and validated in the most incredibly glorious way possible: "Christ has indeed been raised from the dead," Paul proclaims, and it's the most thrilling and affirming part of the good news; for "if Christ has not been raised, your faith is futile; you are still in your sins."[90]

Precisely and only because of Christ's death and resurrection, there can be no more condemnation for sin for us who believe: "Who is to condemn? Christ Jesus is the one who died—more than that, who was raised—who is at the right hand of God, who indeed is interceding for us."[91] Nothing in all creation is more steeped in the miraculous than the fact of your forgiveness and mine.

In the last twenty-four hours alone, I've sinned more than enough to be justly judged by God. But instead of condemning me, He forgives me. And that forgiveness is derived only from that One suspended between heaven and earth in utter abandonment from God.

God, in abandoning His Son, is treating Jesus as a sinner so that He can treat you and me—who *are* sinners—as if we were righteous…all because of Jesus.

CHAPTER NINE

WHAT GOD UNDERSTANDS

His Presence in Our Suffering

The God on whom we rely knows what suffering is all about—
not merely in the way that God knows everything, but by experience.

D. A. CARSON

Years ago, I was with a pastor who told me of a man in his church who one day was cleaning his gun with his son. The unthinkable happened—the gun went off, and the little boy was accidentally killed.

This pastor prayed in desperation as he sat with the distraught father, for he was at a loss to know any comfort he could bring. Then he sensed the Lord saying this to him: "Tell him I understand. Tell him I killed My Son—except it wasn't an accident."

Our heavenly Father always understands our suffering, for at Calvary, He knew suffering that infinitely exceeds anything we'll ever encounter.

DARK HOURS

I'm not trying to minimize human suffering. I don't consider myself to have suffered to any great extent, and one of the most humbling experiences I have is to relate to people who are suffering in ways that are unimaginable to me, especially when they come to me for counsel. What can I say? I have so little in my own background to draw upon.

But I do know that in our time of deepest affliction, none of us find comfort by endlessly focusing on that suffering. There's an element of mystery in all our suffering, and in this life we can't fully understand it, yet we face a subtle temptation to relive and review our suffering. That's an exercise that will never bring rest and release. What *will* bring rest and release is spending more time meditating on the cross and the God of the cross.

So I point to the cross of Christ, for there's no greater encouragement, and no greater motivation for everything God has called you to do and experience in life, than to recognize His love for you in *His* darkest hour, and to receive His care for you in *your* darkest hour.

Those dark times of temptation, trial, and hardship are inevitable for you and for me and for everyone we love. As D. A. Carson points out, all you have to do is live long enough and you'll suffer. You and I and every Christian we know will eventually suffer, if we haven't already; it's an unavoidable experience in a fallen world.[92] But in Gethsemane and at Calvary, we find what we need to prepare ourselves for suffering and to sustain us in suffering.

It's a preparation that braces us for those abrupt announcements that come so unexpectedly:

You're being laid off at work.

The test came back…you've got cancer.

Your baby—I'm sorry, he's dead.

It's a fallen world, and therefore we will all suffer. So we must prepare, because the ideal time to be educated about suffering is never in the midst of it. We need to be trained *prior to* suffering, so that we may be fully sustained *in* suffering.

INCOMPARABLE SOURCE

However, as we look to the cross and Gethsemane for this preparation, there's a distinction we need to make: Our suffering does not truly compare to His.

Occasionally people speak of their "Gethsemane experience." But you and I will never go through anything like what Jesus did at Gethsemane, and we're respectful and wise never to refer to our experiences in those terms. You and I will never be given this cup to drink.

> *We'll never go through anything like what Jesus did at Gethsemane.*

Moreover, you and I have never been, and will never be, abandoned by God. I know sometimes it feels that He's abandoned us; I've felt that way. But those are deceptive feelings, because the One who drank this cup says to you and me, "I will never leave you nor forsake you."[93] We may occasionally feel alone, but we never truly are alone.

And yet His suffering does become the highest and best source of comfort in our own distress. For if He endured so much more than I'll ever have to, then can't He comfort me in my lesser suffering? Yes, absolutely.

So we read Hebrews 4:16 with new appreciation: "Let us then with confidence draw near to the throne of grace, that we may receive mercy and find grace to help in time of need"—in our own dark hour of suffering.

ALWAYS ENOUGH

We notice in Scripture that at the close of Christ's agony in Gethsemane, God sent an angel to Jesus to strengthen Him. Alexander Whyte, the famous Scottish preacher of the 1800s, once said that in heaven, once he'd seen Christ, he wanted his next conversation there to be with this angel. "Who knows," Whyte explained, "what depths of suffering this angel came to witness?"

But in our own depths of suffering, the Father doesn't send an angel; He sends us the *Savior*. In our trials, we're given comfort and strength *by Jesus Himself*.

In our trials, we're given comfort and strength by Jesus Himself.

The first physician to die of AIDS in the United Kingdom was a young Christian who had contracted the virus while doing medical research in Zimbabwe. In his final days, his powers of communication began to fail him. He struggled with increasing difficulty to express his thoughts to his wife, and on one occasion his wife simply could not understand his message.

The young man took a notepad and with a faltering hand wrote the letter *J.*

His wife ran through her mental dictionary several words beginning with J, but none was right.

Then she said to her husband, "Jesus?"

That was the right word.

Jesus was with them. That was all either of them needed to know. *Because that's always enough.*

Regardless of how dark a day becomes, regardless of the severity of the anguish we'll experience, *He's always present...*and *that is sufficient.* The One at God's right hand, the One who on this earth suffered so uniquely, is the One who "always lives to make intercession" for us.[94]

"We little know," Spurgeon writes, "what we owe to our Savior's prayers. When we reach the hilltops of heaven, and look back upon all the way whereby the Lord our God hath led us, how we shall praise Him who, before the eternal throne, undid the mischief which Satan was doing upon earth. How shall we thank Him because He never held His peace, but day and night pointed to the wounds upon His hands, and carried our names upon His breastplate!"[95]

Even in the glory of heaven, the wounds of the Lamb who was slain will continue to bring blessing our way...just as they will now in our own darkest hours on earth.

CHAPTER TEN

ASSURANCE AND JOY

Enjoying the Results of a Cross Centered Life

Nothing in my hand I bring;
Simply to your cross I cling.
AUGUSTUS TOPLADY

It was a Monday morning, and as I stepped toward my office, I saw Melody, one of the secretaries. Melody is a joy and a gem—energy and enthusiasm personified. There's never anything calm about what she's doing or saying.

Melody also has cancer—and she's bald from chemotherapy treatments.

On that Monday morning, Melody greeted me with even more enthusiasm than normal. "Oh, C. J.," she was saying, "Yesterday, yesterday…"

The day before was the long-anticipated Sunday where our church took up a special offering in support of our mission fund. In preparation for it, we'd gone through a month-long time of teaching about our church's mission, as well as instruction about giving. The members of Covenant Life Church in Gaithersburg, Maryland—where I've served for twenty-seven years—are remarkable in how they've always given heroically and joyfully, and now we were asking them to give even more.

When that Sunday came for the special offering, the mood throughout the congregation was one of thrilling excitement. In the lobby where I greet people, I was almost mobbed by those who wanted to express their support and anticipation for this privilege of giving. They were so glad this day had come (and their excitement made me wonder how many pastors ever have such an experience).

Now on this Monday morning, Melody was still glowing from how we all had experienced God's grace. She was getting tears in her eyes. "What a great Sunday in the history of this church," she told me. "Thank you for giving us this opportunity to give!"

I stood there feeling so humbled, feeling I was on holy ground. Melody has spent many days lying sick in bed and looking death in the eye. But there's a joy in her heart and a power from God upon her that I can only behold and envy and rejoice in.

What explains that joy, that power?

Melody has contemplated what happened at Gethsemane. So when you talk with her about suffering, it's the Savior's suffering on her behalf that she's more aware of than any adversity she's experienced. Melody's also aware that because of the Savior's unique suffering for her on the cross, she's deriving indescribable comfort from Him. And what she finds is a new song in her heart that's ultimately for God's praise and His glory.

It's the gospel that sustains Melody with personal assurance of God's grace and love. She has discovered something that the prophet Habakkuk came to know. When life did not make sense to Habakkuk, when all he saw on the horizon was appalling and dreadful suffering for himself and God's people, he responded this way: "Yet I will rejoice in the LORD; I will take joy in the God of my salvation."[96] He turned his attention away from suffering and fixed it upon the more vital issue of salvation.

In your own times of severe distress, which are you more aware of—your suffering or your salvation? What the Puritan Thomas Watson recognized will always be true for us: "Your sufferings are not so great as your sins: Put these two in the balance, and see which weighs heaviest."[97] We can rejoice in our salvation even amid great affliction when we recognize how much worse we deserve because of our sins.

PERSONAL ASSURANCE OF HIS LOVE

As a pastor, few things affect me more than interacting with those who, unlike Melody, are unaware of God's personal love for *them*. Normally there isn't a week that goes by where I'm not talking with someone who hasn't understood this truth—"Christ loved *me* and gave Himself for *me*"—in personal experience.

Christ loved me...Christ gave Himself for me.

Those words are the apostle Paul's: "I have been crucified with Christ," he wrote. "It is no longer I who live, but Christ who lives in me. And the life I now live in the flesh I live by faith in the Son of God, who loved me and gave himself for me."[98] In his commentary on that verse, Leon Morris says this statement "is for me personally the most moving text in the whole of Scripture."

Australian theologian Peter Jensen notes Paul's significant use in this verse of the past tense—not that "Christ loves me," as we might expect him to say, but that "Christ *loved* me." Paul "could not graduate beyond the Cross of Jesus as the source and power of his religion, as the place at which he gained assurance, as the demonstration beyond any other need of proof of the grace and love of God."[99]

Every Christian has the same privilege of saying those words about the cross and knowing this truth personally: "The Son of God loved *me*...the Son of God gave Himself for *me.*" That's why my heart aches for any believer who lacks the certainty of God's specific, passionate, and personal love.

Sinclair Ferguson says we lack this assurance of His personal grace to us "because we fail to focus on that spot where He has revealed it."[100] And "that spot" is obviously the cross.

The distractions that turn us away from the cross are so incessant and so numerous. But failing to focus on the right spot has serious consequences. So here's my question for you: In the last week, what was your primary preoccupation in life? What was your spiritual focus? Was it on that spot where God most reveals His personal love for you—the cross? Or was it on your own circumstances, your own condition, your own concerns? Was your preoccupation with your personal pursuit of godliness? Growth in godliness must be pursued, but never apart from joyful gratitude for the cross.

That's why in my own spiritual diet—and I recommend this for yours as well—a consistent ingredient is the study of the cross, primarily from Scripture but also from many of the outstanding books that have been written about the cross from a strong biblical perspective.[101] Let there never be a lengthy period of time where you aren't receiving inspiration and instruction related directly to the cross, since that's where we find a fresh, sustaining conviction of His personal love.

Martin Luther once wrote that he taught the gospel "again and again, because I greatly fear that after we have laid our head to rest, it will soon be forgotten and will again disappear." That's my great fear as well—that after hearing about the cross, we'll lay down our heads to rest and quietly forget it, instead of dwelling upon it and deriving the continual strength and assurance we need.

Will we lay down our heads tonight and quietly forget the cross?

We have a constant tendency to stop remembering the cross, and to start depending on legalism and self-effort. The danger is relentless. So I urge you every day to "preach the gospel to yourself," as Jerry Bridges calls it in his book *The Discipline of Grace.* Doing so, he says, means "you continually face up to your own sinfulness and then flee to Jesus through faith in His shed blood and righteous life."[102]

By preaching to ourselves the gospel, we easily accept Spurgeon's pithy observation: "Jesus is 'mighty to save,' the best proof of which lies in the fact that He has saved you."[103]

Cultivating Joy

And the inevitable result of preaching the gospel to yourself will be a pronounced joy, an infectious joy, a consistent joy.

Like nothing else, the gospel creates joy; it's both the source and the object of our joy. The gospel alone allows us to obey the biblical directive to "serve the LORD with gladness."[104] Joy is a command. You may be working hard and serving the Lord faithfully, but if you aren't serving with gladness, you aren't serving Him appropriately or representing Him accurately.[105]

> *Like nothing else, the gospel creates joy; it's both the source and the object of our joy.*

Are you someone who's consistently joyful and continually aware that "the joy of the LORD is your strength"?[106] Or do you normally appear to others to be someone who's burdened, busy, and easily bothered?

When the disciples returned to Jesus after a successful ministry trip and reported excitedly, "Lord, even the demons are subject to us in your name!" Jesus responded, "Do not rejoice in this, that the spirits are subject to you, but rejoice that your names are written in heaven."[107] He wasn't trying to minimize the joy one derives from ministry success. But He was drawing their attention away from that to *primary* joy—a joy that takes precedence over the experience of spiritual power. And that is the joy that comes from the gospel, the gospel that writes our names in heaven.

If you're centering your life on the gospel and the cross—if you're abiding hard by the cross, as Spurgeon says, and searching the mystery of Christ's wounds—then you'll be captured by joy. And in these days or years you have left on earth, what could be better?

So cultivate this joy...by continually meditating on the gospel. Let the cross always be the treasure of your heart, your best and highest thought...and your passionate preoccupation.

CHAPTER ELEVEN

BREAKING THE RULE OF LEGALISM

How the Cross Rescues You from the Performance Trap

How easily we fall into the trap of assuming
that we remain justified only so long as there are
grounds in our character for justification.

SINCLAIR FERGUSON

In this book's introduction I mentioned three main tendencies
in particular that tend to draw us away from the gospel and a
cross centered life:

1. Subjectivism, which means basing our view of God on
our changing feelings and emotions.

2. Legalism, which means basing our relationship with God
on our own performance.

3. Condemnation, which means being more focused on our
sin than on God's grace.

Several chapters ago we looked at that first tendency, subjectivism, when we examined God's divine order. We discussed the danger of a feelings-first orientation in evaluating truth, and this helped us begin our exploration of the cross with the right focus.

Now it's time to tackle those other two obstacles.

There's no doubt that one of the greatest hindrances to keeping the gospel central in our lives is our creeping tendency toward legalism. It's an age-old foe to God's plan of salvation through faith alone. From the earliest days of the church, legalism has sidetracked Christians and thrown them off course. And it happens today as much as ever.

Legalism isn't just a matter of someone who has higher standards or more rules than you have. A lot of us wrongly stereotype a legalistic person as someone who never goes to movies or who thinks any music with a beat is evil. Legalism is much more subtle and serious than that—and far more pervasive than most of us realize.

Here's a simple definition I use: Legalism is seeking to achieve forgiveness from God and justification before God through obedience to God.

A legalist is anyone who behaves as if they can earn God's forgiveness through personal performance.

ROOTED IN SELF-WORSHIP

The subtle and serious error of legalism is a sinful fruit from sinful roots.

Thomas Schreiner writes that "legalism has its origin in

self-worship. If people are justified through their obedience to the law, then they merit praise, honor, and glory. Legalism, in other words, means the glory goes to people rather than God."[108]

That's how serious legalism is. The implications are staggering, because legalism claims in essence that the death of Jesus on the cross was either unnecessary or insufficient. It says to God, in effect, "Your plan didn't work. The cross wasn't enough and I need to add my good works to it to be saved."

Of course, no Christian would dare utter such terrible words. But that's the message we send when we shift our concentration away from the gospel, and it represents the height of arrogance in light of God's holiness and my sinfulness.

> *Legalism is ultimately for the purpose of self-worship.*

Legalism is essentially self-atonement for the purpose of self-glorification and ultimately for self-worship. It is the pinnacle of pride for me to assume that by my good works I could ever morally obligate God to forgive me, justify me, or accept me.

We tend to make light of whatever legalistic tendencies we recognize in ourselves because we're actually very comfortable with them. We confess legalistic temptations and tendencies with casualness, and we think, *It's really no big deal.*

That would change if we recognized and confessed those tendencies for what they really are—if in regard to some legalistic action or attitude we honestly admitted, "What this means is that I'm pursuing self-atonement, because I want self-glorification, and ultimately it's all for the purpose of self-worship."

Legalism could not be more serious! No wonder Paul cries out "O foolish Galatians!" when he reproves them for their prideful legalism.[109] This was not a personal insult; the Galatian believers were, in fact, quite intelligent. The issue with the Galatians was not lack of intelligence, but a serious deficiency in spiritual discernment. And if they were vulnerable to the danger of legalism, be assured that so are you and I!

It is in fact a danger that we'll never outgrow in this lifetime. The tendency for legalism exists for each of us each and every day—because of the pride and self-righteousness of our indwelling sin.

Do you therefore know how to discern legalism's presence in your life?

SPINNING PLATES

They probably don't have this on TV anymore, but when I was a kid I remember watching variety shows that sometimes included a popular act known as the Plate Spinner—a guy who balanced several plates atop long flexible rods and kept them all spinning. One by one he would carefully position each plate on a rod and give it a furious spin, until the stage was transformed into a small forest of plates, wiggling and swaying on their sticks.

By the time eight or ten plates were in motion, the first plate was slowing down and wobbling dangerously. The spinner would rush over and, with remarkably skilled hands, instantly return the plate to top-speed rotation. Then on to rescue another wobbling plate, then another and another.

Running back and forth in a flurry of activity, somehow he always got there in time.

That's a helpful picture of how legalism can hijack a Christian. The life of a legalist can become just as frenetic as the plate spinner's performance.

The plates we spin are various spiritual activities—such as Bible reading, prayer, or sharing the gospel—that are good and vital in themselves when pursued for the right reasons.

But often without realizing it, we allow a dangerous shift to take place in our mind and heart. We change what God intends as a means of *experiencing* grace into a means of *earning* grace. Instead of being a further expression of our confidence in God's saving work in our life, these spiritual activities become simply more spinning plates to maintain.

When Sunday morning comes, we'll sing and praise God in church with evident sincerity and zeal when we've had a really good week—with not a single plate wobbling.

But on another Sunday, following a week in which several plates crashed, we're hesitant to approach God and find it difficult to worship freely. We can't escape the feeling that God disapproves of us. Our confidence is no longer in the gospel; it's based instead on our own performance, and when that performance slides, so does our peace and joy.

Are you often more aware of your sin than of the cross?

Do you see such signs of legalism in your own life? Do you often find that you're more aware of your sin than of what Jesus accomplished at the cross? Do you think of God as disappointed with you rather than delighting over you?

Do you lack holy joy? Do you look to your spinning plates for the confidence—indeed, even the right—to approach God?

If you answer yes to any of those questions, you've probably begun to live under the tyranny of legalism.

But don't let this discourage you. God wants to rescue you from the joyless futility of plate spinning through a right understanding of the gospel.

JUSTIFIED: THE FINISHED WORK

In case you're wondering, breaking free from legalism doesn't mean you stop reading your Bible, praying, or sharing the gospel. If you and I want to grow in our faith, we need to take advantage of the tools God gives us in these important spiritual pursuits. The issue is our motive and our understanding of what it means to be saved by grace.

Remember what happened the day you first repented of your sins and trusted in Jesus Christ? In that moment, you were justified, or declared righteous, before God, just as sacred Scripture tells us: In God's sight, "the one who has faith in Jesus" has been *justified by his grace as a gift, through the redemption that is in Christ Jesus."*[110]

That word *justified* is important. It refers to your status before God. When you put your faith in Jesus, God the judge hands down the verdict that you are righteous. He transfers the perfect, sinless record of Jesus to you.

This is amazing grace at its most amazing. In the moment

that you first believed, your past sin didn't cease to exist. You hadn't done any good work that could somehow make up for your disobedience. Yet God completely and totally forgave you. He not only wiped the record of your sin away, He credited the righteousness of His Son to you.

SANCTIFIED: THE ONGOING WORK

However, the power of the gospel doesn't end when we're justified. When God declares a sinner righteous, He immediately begins the process of making that sinner more like His Son.

Through the work of His Spirit, through the power of His Word and involvement with the local church, God peels away our desires for sin, renews our minds, and changes our lives. This ongoing work is what we call "sanctification."

Sanctification is a process—the process of becoming more like Christ, of growing in holiness.

Sanctification is a process—the process of becoming more like Christ, of growing in holiness. This process begins the instant you're converted and won't end until you meet Jesus face-to-face.

Sanctification is about our obedience. It involves work. Empowered by God's Spirit, we strive. We fight sin. We study Scripture and pray, even when we don't feel like it. We flee temptation. We press on; we run hard in the pursuit of holiness. And as we become more and more sanctified, the power of the gospel conforms us more and more closely, with ever-increasing clarity, to the image of Jesus Christ.

DON'T CONFUSE THE TWO

Do you have a clear grasp of what justification and sanctification are? Without understanding the distinction between the two, you'll be vulnerable to legalism. I encourage you to study these theological terms, not so you can impress your friends, but because understanding the differences between justification and sanctification is vital to defeating legalism.

Nearly every person I've met who has struggled with legalism has had a faulty understanding of how justification and sanctification are related to each other and how they're distinct. We must distinguish between justifying grace and sanctifying grace.

At the risk of repeating myself, let's compare them point-by-point so you can clearly see the differences between them:

- Justification is being *declared* righteous.
  Sanctification is being *made* righteous—being conformed to the image of Christ.

- Justification is our *position* before God, a position that becomes permanently ours at the time of our conversion.
  Sanctification is our *practice* that continues throughout our life on earth.

- Justification is *immediate* and complete upon conversion. You'll never be more justified than you are the first moment you trust in the Person and finished work of Christ.

Sanctification is a progressive *process.* You'll be more sanctified as you continue in grace-motivated obedience.

- Justification is *objective*—Christ's work *for* us. Sanctification is *subjective*—Christ's work *within* us.

William Plumer sums it up well when he writes, "Justification is an act. It's not a work, or a series of acts. It's not progressive. The weakest believer and the strongest saint are alike equally justified. Justification admits no degrees. A man is either wholly justified or wholly condemned in the sight of God."[111]

THE LEGALIST'S MISTAKE

Legalists, however, confuse their own ongoing participation in the process of sanctification with God's finished work in justification. They assume that godly practices and good works somehow contribute to their justification. But God's Word is clear: "For by works of the law no human being will be justified in his sight."[112] None of us earn God's approval and love by our good works. None of us can add to the finished, complete work of Jesus on the cross. He paid the price of our sins. He satisfied God's wrath.

Our participation in the process of sanctification comes only after we've been justified before God—by grace alone, through faith alone in Christ alone.

So yes, we work hard at obeying God's Word. We read our Bibles. We pray. We fast. We memorize and meditate on Scripture. We share the gospel. We serve in our church. God commands us in His Word to do many things, and our obedience to them is both pleasing to Him and brings His blessing to our lives.

But not one of these good spiritual activities adds to our justification. We're never "more saved" or "more loved" by God. Our work is motivated by the grace God has poured out in our lives.

Put Down Your Plates

"Our greatest temptation and mistake," writes Sinclair Ferguson, "is to try to smuggle character into God's work of grace."[113] That's the mistake of legalistic plate spinners. In their self-righteous pride, they allow their performance of spiritual duties to become their preoccupation, and in doing so they unwittingly walk away from the main thing—the gospel.

I know the temptation to legalism. That's why, when I complete my daily devotions and close my Bible, I make a point of reminding myself that Jesus' work, not mine, is the basis of my forgiveness and acceptance by God.

I pray, "Lord, I ask for Your grace and strength as I seek to serve You today. I thank You that all Your blessings flow to me from Your Son's work on my behalf. I'm justified by Your grace alone. None of my efforts to obey You and grow in sanctification add to Your finished work at the cross."

What joy the gospel gives me! I can approach the throne of God with confidence—not because I've done a good job at my spiritual duties, but because I'm clothed in the righteousness of Jesus Christ.

God wants you to have this same confidence. He's not impressed with your spinning plates. So renounce all self-righteousness. Make your boast the achievement and work of your substitute and Savior, Jesus Christ.

CHAPTER TWELVE

UNLOADING CONDEMNATION

How the Cross Removes Guilt and Shame

All the love and the acceptance which perfect obedience
could have obtained of God, belong to you—
because Christ was perfectly obedient on your behalf.

CHARLES SPURGEON

I rarely read the comics in the newspaper, but a few years ago someone showed me one I had to keep. It's from a strip called Cathy. Cathy appears to be a single woman in her thirties. In this particular cartoon she's sitting at home, alone with her thoughts.

Things I should have done at work, she thinks to herself. Things I wish I'd said to Irving. Things I promised myself to never do again but I did anyway. Ways I made myself miserable that I could have avoided.

Her look of depression deepens.

Things I could have done for my family, my puppy, my

friends, my coworkers, my neighbor, my finances, my home, my closets, my diet, and millions of people in need whom I've never met.

In the final frame, Cathy summarizes her plight. "Even when I'm not going anywhere, I have three hundred pounds of luggage with me."

CHECK YOUR BAGS

It's amazing how close to home a comic strip can strike. Like Cathy, we can all generate a depressing list of things undone, unsaid, and unaccomplished. Even when we're not going anywhere we can carry hundreds of pounds of luggage.

The Bible calls this luggage "condemnation." At one time or another we all find ourselves carrying some, whether big or small.

Condemnation appears in innumerable forms. It's the weight on the heart of the businessman who was rarely home when his kids were growing up. It's the undercurrent of grief and mental self-torture in the woman who had an abortion years ago. It's the nagging conscience of the Christian man who just muttered a crude insult at a reckless driver. It's the lingering sense of regret over a lack of prayer; it's kind words unsaid and promises broken.

Some of us have been carrying so much for so long that we think it's normal to go through life weighed down. And the truth is that, apart from the cross, condemnation *is* normal. Without Jesus, we all deserve to be condemned and punished for sin. But here's the good news: "There is therefore now no condemnation for those who are in Christ Jesus."[114]

We don't have to go through life under condemnation. In this chapter I want to show you how to unload this crippling burden by embracing the forgiveness offered by the gospel.

LOW-GRADE GUILT

Condemnation is something we all deal with at one time or another in different degrees. It's a mistake to think condemnation is a problem only for people who have committed "major" sins. We can become condemned over any sin, great or small, past or present. The common element is a sustained sense of guilt or shame over sins for which you have repented to God and to any appropriate individuals.

Are you allowing condemnation into your own life? Ask yourself the following questions:

- Do you relate to God as if you were on a kind of permanent probation, suspecting that at any moment He may haul you back into the jail cell of His disfavor?
- When you come to worship do you maintain a "respectful distance" from God, as if He were a fascinating but ill-tempered celebrity known for lashing out at His fans?
- When you read Scripture, does it reveal the boundless love of the Savior or merely intensify your condemnation?
- Are you more aware of your sin than you are of God's grace, given to you through the cross?

Do you see any traces of condemnation in your life? Don't be surprised if you do. But don't keep carrying the burden! Because of the gospel's power you can be completely free of all condemnation.

Not mostly free; *completely* free.

Don't buy the lie that cultivating condemnation and wallowing in your shame is somehow pleasing to God, or that a constant, low-grade guilt will somehow promote holiness and spiritual maturity.

It's just the opposite! *God is glorified when we believe with all our hearts that those who trust in Christ can never be condemned.* It's only when we receive His free gift of grace and live in the good of total forgiveness that we're able to turn from old, sinful ways of living and walk in grace-motivated obedience.

AN UNINVITED GUEST

The Bible records the story of a very unusual dinner party that Jesus attended at the home of Simon the Pharisee. Imagine yourself there in this very tense and powerful scene.[115]

Don't buy the lie that wallowing in your shame is pleasing to God.

We're not told why Jesus has been invited to this dinner, but we know tensions are high between Him and the Pharisees. His host has rudely and conspicuously withheld from Jesus some basic social courtesies that are due a dinner guest: a kiss of greeting, washed feet, a drop of anointing oil. These glaring omissions are obvious to all present.

Suddenly an unexpected person appears. Into the room

comes a known prostitute, a woman despised by polite society.

What happens next is unthinkable to those watching. As Jesus reclines at the low table, leaning on one elbow, His feet stretched out away from the table, the woman stands over Him and begins to weep.

All conversation ceases.

The sound of her weeping grows in volume, filling the house and spilling out into the street. Her freely flowing tears wet His unwashed feet. She kneels, lets down her hair, and with it begins to wipe Jesus' feet. She kisses them and anoints them with perfume as an act of worship.

Can you feel the atmosphere in that room? No one eats. No one moves. Perhaps strangest of all, Jesus does nothing to suggest that the shocking behavior of this sinful woman is anything but appropriate.

OUR MANY SINS

I believe God recorded this dramatic event in Scripture for a specific purpose: He wants us to see ourselves in that woman and follow her example.

The woman who washed Jesus' feet with her tears was someone who had repented of her sins. This isn't her first encounter with Jesus; no doubt she'd listened to Him teach and found in His words the hope for forgiveness and cleansing no one else was willing to grant her.

When we meet her, she has already believed in Jesus and turned away from her old life. This isn't the account of her salvation; rather, this is a beautiful expression of Christian worship born of her love, adoration, and thankfulness toward her Savior. She recognizes her sin and unworthiness, and weeps deeply.

Her tears, however, are not tears of condemnation. She weeps because her guilt is gone. She loves much because she's been forgiven much. These are tears of joy, gratitude, and extravagant devotion.

LOSE YOUR LUGGAGE

The Christian who desires to live a cross centered life will regularly face his or her own depravity and the seriousness of personal sin, and he or she will do it squarely and unflinchingly. Our sinfulness is a reality. But the reality of the death and resurrection of Jesus for the forgiveness of sin is even greater.

This doesn't mean we won't struggle occasionally with condemnation. On a daily basis, the luggage of condemnation will show up on our doorstep, begging us to load it onto our backs. In opposition to God, our pride will tell us that Jesus' sacrifice couldn't possibly be enough to secure the Father's favor completely, unreservedly, and forever.

It's impossible to resolve issues of yesterday by doing better tomorrow.

Do you see the luggage piling up? The enemy of our soul with his lies will always be swift to whisper these accusations.

When these challenges come, don't try to fight condemnation by promising to pray more, or fast more often, or memorize more Scripture. Future obedience is certainly important, but it's impossible to resolve issues of yesterday by doing better tomorrow. Our promises of future obedience, however sincere, can't resolve condemnation for past sin.

BEATING CONDEMNATION

Here's how to beat condemnation: Confess your sin to God…then believe in Him. Exercise the gift of faith God has given you to believe that Jesus died for the very sins you're feeling condemned for.

The punishment He received was for you. His resurrection is proof that God accepted Jesus' sacrifice. The sins of your distant past as well as your sins of yesterday were all atoned for; you need carry their weight no more.

You *can't* atone for your sin. That's why Jesus did it for you.

Being freed from condemnation doesn't require that we forget or deny the depth and depravity of our sins, whether they're committed prior to our conversion or since our conversion. In fact, if we want to know the joy and gratitude that the woman at Jesus' feet experienced, we must start by acknowledging and owning up to our many sins.

Though Paul called himself the "foremost" of sinners,[116] he wasn't paralyzed by condemnation; he was exalting God's grace by recognizing his own unworthiness and sin as he marveled at the mercy of God.

Every one of us can honestly claim the title "worst of sinners"; it isn't specially reserved for the Adolf Hitlers of the world. "We may justly condemn ourselves as the greatest sinners we know," writes William Law, "because we know more of the folly of our own heart than we do of other people's."[117]

So admit it: You're the worst sinner you know. Admit you're unworthy and deserve to be condemned.

But don't stop there! Move on to rejoicing in the Savior who came to save the worst of sinners. Lay down the luggage of condemnation and kneel in worship at the feet of Him who bore your sins. Cry tears of amazement.

And confess with Paul: "I was shown mercy so that in me, the worst of sinners, Christ Jesus might display his unlimited patience as an example for those who would believe on him and receive eternal life."[118]

CHAPTER THIRTEEN

THE CROSS CENTERED DAY

Practical Ways to Focus Daily on the Cross

The traveler through the Bible landscape misses his way as
soon as he loses sight of the hill called Calvary.

J. I. PACKER

We humans are creatures of habit, aren't we? And our habits
reflect our true selves—we all build our daily lives around our
priorities and passions.

Visit the same coffee shop a few mornings in a row and
you'll see what I'm talking about. Each day the same people
repeat the same routine over and over.

I'm sure you have your own daily rituals. Reading the
sports page of the *Washington Post* each day became one of
mine. I count it a good day when I find the time to sit down,
read my favorite sports columnists, and get the latest scores and
stats. Add some chocolate to the routine and it becomes a *very*
good day!

We make time for what we truly value. We build habits and routines around the things that really matter to us. This is an important principle to understand as we seek to build our lives around the gospel.

A cross centered life is made up of cross centered days.

Do you want to live a cross centered life? A cross centered life is made up of *cross centered days.*

And those days are ones in which we stay near enough to the cross "for its sparks to fall on us," to return again to that John Stott quotation; we don't let ourselves forget that the cross of Christ "is the blazing fire at which the flame of our love is kindled."[119]

How do you keep the flame of gospel passion burning brightly in the drizzle of real life? Let me share some simple ways I've found to help me receive the "sparks" of the cross each day.

PREACH TO YOURSELF

Reminding ourselves of the gospel is the most important daily habit we can establish. If the gospel is the most vital news in the world, and if salvation by grace is the defining truth of our existence, we should create ways to immerse ourselves in these truths every day. No days off allowed.

This is "preaching the gospel to yourself," as we earlier learned about from Jerry Bridges. And don't worry—even if you don't consider yourself a public speaker, you can do this kind of preaching. Your audience is your own heart. And the message is simple: Christ died for your sins.

It's a matter of sitting down, grabbing your own attention, and telling yourself, "Hey, listen up! This is what matters most: You're forgiven! You have hope! Your hope is based on the sacrifice of Jesus. So let's not view this day any other way. Let today be governed by this *one defining truth.*"

But let's be practical. How do you maintain your cross centeredness in the midst of a busy schedule amid the demands of work and family? Let me share five very simple ways I've found that help me draw near to the cross each day.

1. MEMORIZE THE GOSPEL

God instructs us in the Psalms to store up His Word in our hearts.[120] I love that picture. God wants us to tuck His promises into our hearts so that, no matter where we are or what we're doing, we can pull them out and be strengthened by their truth.

You might not think you're good at memorizing Scripture. That's okay. Don't give up. Work at it. God isn't keeping score. Even if it takes you longer than someone else, it's worth the effort.

And if you're already memorizing Scripture, practice what my friend Mike Bullmore calls "strategic Scripture memory." Start with passages that define and describe the gospel. All God's promises and commands are precious and powerful, but those verses (like the ones mentioned below) that tell us of the Son of God who gave His life in our place are the most precious and powerful of all. Since you have to begin somewhere in

Scripture memory, why not start with the Bible's central message?

Having these verses instantly accessible is so helpful. If you find yourself losing perspective in the midst of life's daily troubles and inconveniences, reach into your memory and pull out this verse:

2 Corinthians 5:21

> For our sake he made him to be sin who knew no sin, so that in him we might become the righteousness of God.

If you're struggling with condemnation over a sin that you've repented of and turned away from, reflect on this passage:

Romans 8:31–34

> If God is for us, who can be against us? He who did not spare his own Son but gave him up for us all, how will he not also with him graciously give us all things? Who shall bring any charge against God's elect? It is God who justifies. Who is to condemn? Christ Jesus is the one who died—more than that, who was raised—who is at the right hand of God, who indeed is interceding for us.

Here are more key passages that speak of God's work of salvation through the cross. You're probably familiar with some or all of these, but let me encourage you to read and reflect on them again—and to store them in your heart:

Isaiah 53:3–6

He was despised and rejected by men; a man of sorrows, and acquainted with grief; and as one from whom men hide their faces he was despised, and we esteemed him not. Surely he has borne our griefs and carried our sorrows; yet we esteemed him stricken, smitten by God, and afflicted. But he was wounded for our transgressions; he was crushed for our iniquities; upon him was the chastisement that brought us peace, and with his stripes we are healed. All we like sheep have gone astray; we have turned every one to his own way; and the LORD has laid on him the iniquity of us all.

Romans 3:23–26

For all have sinned and fall short of the glory of God, and are justified by his grace as a gift, through the redemption that is in Christ Jesus, whom God put forward as a propitiation by his blood, to be received by faith. This was to show God's righteousness, because in his divine forbearance he had passed over former sins. It was to show his righteousness at the present time, so that he might be just and the justifier of the one who has faith in Jesus.

Romans 5:6–11

For while we were still weak, at the right time Christ died for the ungodly. For one will scarcely die for a righteous person—though perhaps for a good person one would dare even to die—but God shows his love for us in that while we were still sinners, Christ died for us. Since, therefore, we have now been justified by his blood, much more shall we be saved by him from the wrath of God. For if while we were enemies we were reconciled to God by the death of his Son, much more, now that we are reconciled, shall we be saved by his life. More than that, we also rejoice in God through our Lord Jesus Christ, through whom we have now received reconciliation.

1 Corinthians 15:3–4

For I delivered to you as of first importance what I also received: that Christ died for our sins in accordance with the Scriptures, that he was buried, that he was raised on the third day in accordance with the Scriptures.

Galatians 2:21

I do not nullify the grace of God, for if justification were through the law, then Christ died for no purpose.

If your interaction with the Word of God is not consistently making you more aware of the cross—getting you near enough to allow the sparks of this blazing fire to fall on you— then focus your attention specifically on such gospel passages as those listed here. And the result of this exercise is that your heart will become more sensitized to see the powerful presence of the gospel throughout Scripture.

2. PRAY THE GOSPEL

The gospel should be at the center of your prayer life because it makes it possible for us to approach God. The gospel gives us the confidence to pray boldly—we're accepted in God's beloved Son.

There's nothing complicated about this. To pray the gospel, simply begin by thanking God for the forgiveness of sins, purchased through the death of His Son. Acknowledge that Christ's work on the cross is what makes prayer possible.

Thank Him that you'll never be separated from God's love

because Jesus bore God's wrath for sin. Thank Him that because of the cross you're reconciled to God and have been given the Holy Spirit to dwell in you, lead you, guide you, and empower you to resist sin and serve God. Then ask God to bless you graciously with everything you need to obey and glorify Him.

The gospel should be woven throughout our praise, our petitions, and our intercession, because our approach to God the Father is only—ever and always—through God the Son and His work on the cross.

3. SING THE GOSPEL

I'm no singer (ask my friends), but I love to sing about the cross. A Christian's heart should be brimming over every day with the song of Calvary.

This is another opportunity to be strategic. There are countless worship CDs available, but it's important to choose ones that draw our attention to the amazing truth of what God has done on our behalf. Not all worship songs are created equal; many today are more centered on ourselves than on the cross and on Christ. They focus more on what we need or what we want God to do than on what Jesus has already done.

Many worship songs center more on ourselves than on Christ.

I have to admit I'm spoiled when it comes to great cross centered worship songs. Some of my friends are very gifted songwriters who create beautiful contemporary worship songs that are filled with the gospel. (You can find out more about how to obtain this music—including a CD created specifically in conjunction with this book—at www.sovereigngrace ministries.org.)

Wherever you find it, make cross centered worship a regular part of your daily routine. There's no better way to start each day than to employ songs and hymns that speak of the cross with clarity and power.

Let me share one of my favorites, a classic hymn by John Newton. Please don't skip or rush through the lines as you read. Take them in slowly, and out loud.

In evil long I took delight
    Unawed by shame or fear;
Till a new object struck my sight
    And stopped my wild career.
I saw one hanging on a tree
    In agonies and blood;
Who fixed his languid eyes on me
    As near his cross I stood.
Sure never till my latest breath
    Can I forget that look;
It seemed to charge me with his death
    Though not a word he spoke.
My conscience felt and owned the guilt
    And plunged me in despair;
I saw my sins his blood had spilt
    And helped to nail him there.

Alas, I knew not what I did
    But now my tears are vain;
Where shall my trembling soul be hid?
    For I the Lord have slain.
A second look he gave which said
    "I freely all forgive;
This blood is for thy ransom paid
    I died that thou mayest live."
Thus while his death my sin displays
    In all its blackest hue;
Such is the mystery of grace,
    It seals my pardon too.
With pleasing grief and mournful joy
    My spirit now is filled;
That I should such a life destroy
    Yet live by him I killed.[121]

Do you feel the effect such rich words can have on you? Hymns like these, and many contemporary worship choruses as well—*if they are centered on the cross*—can help you make the gospel the sound track of your day.

4. REVIEW HOW THE GOSPEL HAS CHANGED YOU

Many people today want to forget the past. The mistakes they've made and the sins they've committed aren't subjects they like to revisit. But for Christians, one of the best ways we can draw near the blazing fire of the cross is to remember our past, and allow it to remind us of how marvelous God's salvation really is.

The apostle Paul was committed to remembering what he once was because that memory magnified God's grace. Earlier we quoted Paul's remembrance of being "a blasphemer, persecutor, and insolent opponent" of God, and then his grateful words, "But I received mercy..."[122] Though written some thirty years after he came to faith in Christ, Paul remembered vividly and specifically his many sins prior to conversion. Knox Chamblin writes, "Vital to Paul's effectiveness as an apostle is that he never forgets his day as a persecutor.... An ongoing awareness of grace reminds Paul of the appalling sin from which he has been delivered; an ongoing awareness of sin keeps him dependent on grace."[123]

You didn't write your conversion story by yourself; God intervened to save you from His wrath.

You and I as well must not forget. We need to follow Paul's example. We can all say, "I was once a _____"—and fill in the blank with an accurate description of our sinful past. And we don't need a dramatic testimony to do so. Every conversion is still a miracle of God's grace. You didn't write that story by yourself; God intervened to change your heart and save you from His wrath.

Take time to think about all this. Reflect on it daily. I also encourage you to write out your testimony in a page or two. And don't just write "I asked Jesus into my heart," but really spell out the heart of the gospel and how the blood of Christ, shed for the sins of the world, came to apply to you personally. Be specific about the fact that God is holy and you were an object of His wrath. Identify the sin in which you were lost. Explain how God saved you and changed your life for His glory.

This will edify and encourage you and prepare you to share both your personal testimony and the truth of the gospel with others.

5. STUDY THE GOSPEL

To grow in your *passion* for what Jesus has done, increase your *understanding* of what He has done.

Never be content with your current grasp of the gospel. The gospel is life-permeating, world-altering, universe-changing truth. It has more facets than any diamond. We will never exhaust its depths. So let me share some practical recommendations for making the gospel an ongoing life-study:

- Camp out in the books of Romans and Galatians. Author John Stott, among others, has written excellent commentaries on both to assist you in your study.

- Don't be afraid of technical theological terms. Take the time to learn the meanings of such words as *atonement, substitution, propitiation, justification, redemption, reconciliation,* and *salvation.* If you're looking for a guide, *The Gospel for Real Life* by Jerry Bridges explains each of these words in detail. Understanding them will better help you appreciate and marvel at what God has done.[124]

- If you have a daily commute, or another regular time when you can listen to audio recordings, obtain cross centered sermons that you can hear and benefit from (you'll find some at www.sovereigngraceministries.org).

- Read your whole Bible with your eyes peeled for the gospel. It has been noted that every passage of Scripture —in both the Old and New Testaments—either predicts, prepares for, reflects, or results from the work of Christ. As you read Scripture in your daily devotions, identify how each passage relates to the cross. The Old Testament in particular will come alive as you see it pointing to the coming Savior. For discovering the story line of the gospel throughout Scripture, there is no better guide than the two volumes *For the Love of God* by D. A. Carson.[125]

- Finally, here's a New Year's resolution that's truly worthwhile: Make it an annual goal to read or reread at least one book on the cross. The following list mentions some great books to start with.

    The Cross of Christ by John Stott. A personal favorite. Stott says of the Savior, "It was by his death that he wished above all else to be remembered."[126] This book won't let you forget.

The Discipline of Grace by Jerry Bridges.[127] Another personal favorite. The first three chapters of this book in particular are worth reading and rereading for the rest of your life.

The Power of the Cross of Christ by Charles Spurgeon.[128] My historical hero exhorts us to "abide hard by the cross and search the mystery of his wounds."[129] There's no better human guide for this holy search.

The Cross and Christian Ministry by D. A. Carson.[130] For pastors this is a must-read. I'm indebted to Dr. Carson for this book. It has defined effective pastoral ministry for me, and it will do the same for you.

You Can't Do This on Your Own

I hope these five practical recommendations have given you a clearer understanding of what it means to make every day a day centered on the cross. But remember that we can't do this on our own. We need God's Spirit to light the truths of the cross within our hearts. This is true at the moment our hearts are regenerated, and it continues to be true every day of our Christian lives.

D. A. Carson writes:

There has not only been an objective, public act of divine self-disclosure in the crucifixion of God's own Son, but there must be a private work of God by His Spirit, in the mind and heart of the individual. If we should express unqualified gratitude to God for the gift of His Son, we should express no less gratitude for the gift of the Spirit who enables us to grasp the gospel of His Son.... Unless the Spirit enlightens us, God's thoughts will remain deeply alien to us.[131]

Each time we memorize, pray, sing, review, or study the gospel, we must ask the Holy Spirit to open our eyes and bring the gospel alive to us again. He's quick to hear and faithful to answer. But His help must be actively sought.

Because of the empowering grace of God's Spirit, I've been drawing near the cross day after day for many years now. I haven't done it perfectly, and there are many days when my heart isn't as passionate as it should be, but I can honestly say my appreciation of and passion for the gospel has been growing steadily. The suggestions I've made in this chapter have been invaluable to me in that growing process.

If God can bring about this progress in my life, He can do the same for you. Keep drawing near, and build a cross centered life one day at a time.

CHAPTER FOURTEEN

NEVER MOVE ON

*Put This Book on a Shelf—
But Not Its Message!*

The Spirit does not take his pupils beyond the cross,
but ever more deeply into it.

J. KNOX CHAMBLIN

I was smoking pot the first time I heard the gospel.

I'm a Christian because God showed me mercy, not because I was worthy or wanting to be saved. No, I wasn't searching for God.

God came looking for me.

It was 1972. I was sitting in my bedroom when my friend Bob began sharing the simple story of Jesus dying for my sins, a story I'd never heard despite growing up in a church.

But that night as I listened, God revealed Himself and regenerated my heart. I believed, and I repented. The cross was for *me*. Jesus was *my* Savior.

The worst of sinners, in the midst of his sin, was born again.

That was more than thirty years ago. A lot has changed since then. The long hair has all fallen out. I'm a grandfather. My wife, Carolyn, and I recently celebrated our thirtieth wedding anniversary. And after twenty-seven years as a senior pastor of a church, I've passed along the baton to a younger man.

I've learned a lot over those years. Before that evening when Bob told me the gospel, I literally knew nothing of God or His Word. I'd never cracked open a Bible. But from the day of my conversion I couldn't get enough of Scripture or Christian books. Not long after my conversion, I got a job at a Christian bookstore just so I could read as much as possible.

My love for books hasn't abated. Today the walls of my ministry office are lined with books from floor to ceiling. Sometimes in the midst of my daily responsibilities I'll look up at them, amazed at the difference they've made in my life.

The thousands of titles are a striking visual reminder of the many ideas and messages—many good, some not-so-good—that have vied for my attention over the years. Most of my collection comprises classic books written hundreds of years ago by men like Charles Spurgeon, Jonathan Edwards, and the Puritans. But I also have many books written more recently.

Some are better than others. I could take you to some that represent Christian fads of the past thirty years. At the time, their innovative ideas for personal growth and effective ministry were all the rage. Now they're forgotten.

I keep them because I want a sobering reminder, constantly close to me, of all the off-center messages that might tempt me to move on from the *one message that matters*—the gospel.

I've come a long way since I heard the gospel in a drug-induced high, and I've traveled many miles in this journey of faith. A lot has changed—but a lot has stayed the same. I'm grateful to say that what matters most has remained consistent: *The cross is still at the center.* By His grace I've never moved on from the cross of Jesus Christ, and I never want to.

IT REALLY IS ENOUGH

Here we are at the final chapter of this book. My time with you is about to end. Once you've finished reading a few more pages you'll be done, and you'll place this volume on a bookshelf of your own. Maybe one day in the future you'll pull it out to review a quote or flip through a chapter or two. Or maybe you'll never touch it again.

Don't worry—I won't mind if my book winds up in a forgotten corner of a bookshelf, collecting dust. But I do hope the message of this book is one you'll *never* put on a shelf. Never let the cross slide into second or third place in your life. *Never lay it aside. Never move on.*

I hear you asking, "Don't I need more than the cross?"

I can hear you asking, "But don't I need more than the cross?"

In one sense, the answer is no. Nothing else is of equal importance. The message of Christ and Him crucified is the Christian's hope, confidence, and assurance. Heaven will be spent marveling at the work of Christ, the God-Man who suffered in the place of us sinners.

In another sense, the answer's yes. You do need more. You've been saved to grow, to serve in a local church, to do good works, and to glorify God. But the "more" you need as a follower of Christ won't be found apart from the cross. The gospel isn't one class among many that you'll attend during your life as a Christian—the gospel is the whole building where all the classes take place! Rightly approached, all the topics you'll study and focus on as a believer will be offered to you "within the walls" of the glorious gospel.

Name any area of the Christian life that you want to learn about or that you want to grow in. The Old Testament? The end times? Do you want to grow in holiness or the practice of prayer? To become a better husband, wife, or parent? None of these can be rightly understood apart from God's grace through Jesus' death. They, and indeed all topics, should be studied through the lens of the gospel.

Let me share a few specific examples of what it means to study the following areas through this lens.

THE CROSS AND THE OLD TESTAMENT

Some people are scared of the Old Testament. They find it confusing and hard to understand. Others are fascinated with it for the wrong reasons.

Only the person who understands that the cross is the center of all human history can understand the Old Testament. Through the lens of the gospel, the Bible truly becomes one book telling one story—the story of sinful man, a holy God, and His plan of salvation through the substitution of Himself for His people.

To be a true student of the ancient books of Scripture, we never move on from the gospel. *Everything* in the Old Testament points toward Jesus Christ and enriches our understanding of the cross, just as Jesus Himself explained.[132]

The drama of redemption begins in the Garden of Eden in Genesis 3 and continues to unfold throughout the Old Testament until it reaches its climax at the cross. All along the way, the Divine Author prepares us for Calvary: The symbolism of the sacrificial system, the giving of the law, the repeated failures of man, and the steadfast faithfulness of God—all this and more deepens our amazement at the cross.

For help in gaining a better grasp of the gospel's disclosure throughout the Old Testament, I recommend Graeme Goldsworthy's *According to Plan: The Unfolding Revelation of God in the Bible.*[133]

THE CROSS AND THE END TIMES

In recent decades, countless books have been written about the last days and the final return of Christ. The study of the end times—eschatology—provides limitless possibilities to the human imagination, and has become an especially popular subject for novelists, playing to the conspiracy-theory tendencies in modern man.

What we believe about Christ's return is important, but what is sad is the inordinate amount of attention and energy given to the details of that return balanced against the distinct lack of focus on the saving work of the cross that should stand at the very center of any such discussion.

Regardless of your personal opinion about the Rapture or the Millennium, it's undeniable that in Scripture the work of Christ at Calvary still takes center stage. His Second Coming is the culmination of the victory He accomplished over death and hell at the cross.

Jesus didn't instruct His disciples to concern themselves with the details of when and where He would return. They were to watch and pray, but their primary preoccupation was to be *exulting in and proclaiming the good news of His death and resurrection.*

The cross stays on center stage even when the end times and eternity are portrayed in the New Testament's final book, as Jim Elliff points out: "One is taken aback by the emphasis upon the cross in Revelation. Heaven does not 'get over' the cross, as if there are better things to think about"; heaven is not only Christ-centered, Elliff observes, but cross-centered—"and quite blaring about it."[134]

Because of the cross, history's conclusion is already written: Jesus is victorious, all those who trust in Him have eternal life, and Satan is defeated! No force on earth, no agonies of persecution, can snatch away from Jesus Christ those whom He died to save. Nothing can separate them from His love.

THE CROSS AND PRAYER

Effective prayer is prayer saturated in the gospel. To learn to pray you must become familiar with the Bible's teaching on prayer. You'll want to pray with other godly Christians and learn from their example. But again, you don't move on from the cross to go deeper into prayer. Ultimately, all effective prayer is rooted in the cross.

Think about it. The gospel is the starting point of prayer. Without Christ's blood, you couldn't even approach God. Only in Jesus' righteousness are we invited to enter His presence.

Students in the school of prayer never graduate from the school of the gospel.

There's no mantra we can learn, no catchphrase we can recite, that will move God's hand. We appeal to Him based on the person and work of His Son. "When we pray to God for His blessing," Jerry Bridges writes, "He does not examine our performance to see if we are worthy. Rather, He looks to see if we are trusting in the merit of His Son as our only hope for securing His blessing."[135]

Students in the school of prayer never graduate from the school of the gospel.

THE CROSS AND HOLINESS

Do you want to grow in personal holiness? Maybe there's a particular area of sin you battle that you want to overcome. Here's the temptation you'll face.

Your pride and sinful self-sufficiency will tell you, "Okay, this material about the gospel has been great. But now it's time to put all that grace aside and get down to work. It's time to make some change happen and get holy!"

That's not going to work. Driven by legalistic fervor, you might appear to make progress, but it will be short-lived. Only grace sustains lasting change and sanctification. Through the

cross we overcome not only the guilt of sin, but the power of
sin as well. Because of the cross we can successfully battle and
overcome sinful patterns and practices. The cross motivates us
to be holy as our Father in heaven is holy. The gospel empow-
ers our ongoing pursuit of sanctification.

THE CROSS AND RELATIONSHIPS

What about the practical stuff? Surely there comes a time when
we move on from the gospel just a little so we can focus on the
everyday issues of our relationships with other people.

This is tempting to believe, but it's just not true. Regardless
of your relationship to others, whether you're single or married,
a husband or a wife, a father, a mother, or a grandparent, your
faithfulness and effectiveness in your relationships are directly
tied to your understanding of the cross.

Because of sin, relational conflict is inevitable. You'll sin
against others. They'll sin against you. You'll need to forbear
with others. You'll need to forgive.

Your relationships with others must be based on your relationship to God through the cross. We're commanded in
Scripture, "Be kind and compassionate to one another, forgiv-
ing each other, *just as in Christ God forgave you.*"[136]

When I become bitter or unforgiving toward others, I'm
assuming that the sins of others are more serious than my sins
against God. The cross transforms my perspective. Through the
cross I realize that no sin committed against me will ever be as
serious as the innumerable sins I've committed against God.

When we understand how much God has forgiven us, it's not difficult to forgive others.

God's been patient with me so I can be patient with others. God has forgiven me so I can forgive others. God's grace is changing me so I can trust that He can also change others.

There's so much more that can be said—this is just a brief introduction to the transforming effect of the cross on every one of our relationships. But the point is simple yet powerful. *If you're single, live a cross centered life. If you're married, build a cross centered marriage. If you have children, practice cross centered parenting.* The "practical" stuff flows from the "central" stuff.

BETTER THAN I DESERVE

I mentioned earlier my practice of answering the question "How are you?" with the reply "Better than I deserve." Though at times it seems to convince people that I view myself too negatively, the simple truth is that I understand who I am and where I deserve to be. I deserve God's wrath. Honestly, I deserve to be in hell.

But instead I'm God's adopted child, I'm forgiven of my many sins, and I'm loved by Him! I'm going to heaven! *I'm doing so much better than I deserve.*

That perspective fills me with joy even on days when things aren't going as I planned. We all face disappointments and difficult circumstances; we all experience trials and suffering. But understanding the gospel lets us marvel at God's love regardless of our circumstances.

I don't know what tomorrow holds, but I do know this: Because of the cross, I'll be doing much better than I deserve. That's why, for the rest of my life, I want only to move deeper into the wonderful mystery of God's love for me.

The gospel isn't just for unbelievers. It's for Christians, too. "Every day of our Christian experience," writes Jerry Bridges, "should be a day of relating to God on the basis of His grace alone. We are not only saved by grace, but we also live by grace every day."[137]

This is why the gospel is truly the main thing. This is why it should always be at the center of our lives.

So even though this book is over, don't put its precious truth on the shelf. May the reality of what God has done for you continue to be the most captivating thought in your mind...and may the truth of Christ's death for you always be the most precious treasure in your heart.

SPECIAL THANKS

To Don Jacobson for taking a risk and thinking this might be a good idea.

To Doug Gabbert for convincing Don this might be a good idea.

To Joshua Harris. This was all your idea, my friend! Apart from your initiative and encouragement, I would never have written what has now become this book. And I will never forget that evening when you unexpectedly showed up at my home with your proposal for *The Cross Centered Life*. In the midst of writing your own book with a fast-approaching deadline, and without informing me, you were also working on what has now become this book. I hope it brings you much joy.

To Thomas Womack, for his unique skill in crafting, clarifying, and combining the content of two books, as well as helping me add new material, thus creating a new book. This wouldn't exist apart from the hard work and unique gifting of this humble servant. It has been an honor to work on this book with you, my friend.

To Kevin Meath for his invaluable work on *The Cross Centered Life*. Thanks for first turning my sermons into a manuscript we could begin to work with.

To my daughter Nicole, for her love for her father and for her loving editing of this book.

To Steve Whitacre, Jeff Purswell, Justin Taylor, Bob Kauflin and Brian Chesemore, for your time, helpful editing recommendations, and meaningful encouragement.

To Al Mohler for writing the foreword. What an honor to have the foreword written by one of my heroes in the faith!

To Nora Earles, who is simply the best secretary in the world.

To Covenant Life Church for your kind and consistent support in prayer. For twenty-eight years you've been the dearest people on earth to me, and you made me the happiest pastor on earth.

To my extraordinary wife, Carolyn. There is no one I love or respect more than you.

1. 1 Corinthians 15:1, 3

2. Jerry Bridges, *The Discipline of Grace* (Colorado Springs, CO: NavPress, 1994), 46.

3. D. A. Carson, *The Cross and Christian Ministry: An Exposition of Passages from 1 Corinthians* (Grand Rapids, MI: Baker Books, 1993), 26.

4. John R. W. Stott, *Guard the Gospel* (Downers Grove, IL: InterVarsity Press, 1973), 22.

5. David Prior, *Message of 1 Corinthians: Life in the Local Church* (Downers Grove, IL: InterVarsity Press, 1985), 51.

6. This bit of wisdom appears in many places; it was quoted by U.S. Secretary of Education William J. Bennett, in an address to the National Press Club, Washington, D.C., March 17, 1985.

7. 1 Corinthians 2:2

8. Charles H. Spurgeon, in his sermon "Wherefore Should I Weep?" (October 22, 1876, Metropolitan Tabernacle, London).

9. Scripture quotations in this section are from 2 Timothy 4:5–7; 2:8; and 1:13–14.

10. Carson, *Cross and Christian Ministry*, 38.

11. John Piper, "Only a New Creation Counts," sermon preached at Bethlehem Baptist Church, Minneapolis, August 28, 1983, available online at http://www.desiringgod.org/library/sermons/83/082883.html.

12. 1 Corinthians 2:2

13. J. Knox Chamblin, *Paul and the Self: Apostolic Teaching for Personal Wholeness* (Grand Rapids, MI: Baker Books, 1993), 70.

14. 1 Timothy 1:13–14

15. Psalm 32:2

16. Romans 3:23

17. James 4:6; 1 Peter 5:5

18. Quotations from David Martyn Lloyd-Jones in this section are from an excellent chapter on "Feelings" in his book *Spiritual Depression: Its Causes and Its Cure* (Grand Rapids, MI: Eerdmans, 1965, reprinted 2001).

19. Lloyd-Jones, *Spiritual Depression*, 20.

20. Sinclair B. Ferguson, from a class in Systematic Theology, Reformed Theological Seminary, January 2001.

21. Sinclair B. Ferguson, *Deserted by God?* (Grand Rapids, MI: Baker Books, 1993), 24.

22. Spurgeon recounted this story years later in a sermon entitled "All of Grace," given at London's Metropolitan Tabernacle.

23. Romans 10:17

24. Galatians 3:1

25. Ephesians 3:8

26. Charles H. Spurgeon, *Morning and Evening* (Peabody, MA: Hendrickson Publishers, 1991), January 4, evening meditation.

27. C. S. Lewis, *The Lion, the Witch and the Wardrobe* (New York: Macmillan, 1950), Chapter XV, "Deeper Magic from *Before* the Dawn of Time." Emphasis added.

28. Derek Tidball, *The Message of the Cross* (Downers Grove, IL: InterVarsity Press, 2001), 101.

29. Franz Delitzsch, *Keil and Delitzsch Commentary on the Old Testament: Updated Edition* (Hendrickson Publishers, 1996), introductory comments on Isaiah 53. Originally published in 1866.

30. Isaiah 52:13 (The final three verses in chapter 52 are the opening lines in the prophecy that continues through all of chapter 53.)

31. Isaiah 53:2

32. John 1:46; Mark 6:3

33. Isaiah 53:2

34. Isaiah 53:3

35. Isaiah 53:5

36. Isaiah 51:9; 52:10; 53:1

37. 1 Corinthians 1:22–23

38. Isaiah 52:14

39. Ernest Gordon, *Through the Valley of the Kwai,* republished as *To End All Wars* (Grand Rapids, MI: Zondervan, 2002).

40. Isaiah 53:6

41. Isaiah 53:4

42. Sinclair Ferguson, *Grow in Grace* (Carlisle, Pa.: Banner of Truth, 1989) 56 and 58.

43. Luke 17:11–13

44. 1 Timothy 1:17

45. 1 Timothy 1:9–10

46. 1 Timothy 1:13

47. 1 Timothy 1:15

48. 1 Timothy 2:4

49. Job 9:2, 32 (NIV)

50. Job 9:33–34 (NIV)

51. Hebrews 9:22

52. 1 Timothy 2:5–6

53. J. I. Packer, *God's Words: Studies of Key Bible Themes* (Grand Rapids, MI: Baker, 1998), 109.

54. R. C. Sproul, *Saved from What?* (Wheaton, IL: Crossway Books, 2002).

55. John R. W. Stott, *The Cross of Christ* (Downers Grove, IL: InterVarsity Press, 1986), 159.

56. Ron Rhodes, *Christ before the Manger* (Eugene, OR: Wipf & Stock Publishers, 2002), 205.

57. Mark 14:32

58. Mark 14:33

59. Mark 14:34–35

60. John 13:21

61. Mark 14:27–28 (NIV)

62. Mark 10:32

63. Katherine A. M. Kelly, "Give Me a Sight, O Savior."

64. Mark 14:36

65. Luke 22:44

66. Psalm 11:6

67. Jeremiah 25:16

68. William Lane, *Commentary on the Gospel of Mark* (Grand Rapids, MI: Eerdmans, 1974), 516.

69. Mark 14:41–42

70. Luke 22:43

71. Matthew 27:12–14

72. Mark 10:45
73. Matthew 27:15–17
74. Matthew 27:19
75. Matthew 27:20
76. Matthew 27:21–24
77. Luke 23:23
78. Luke 23:49
79. John 19:25
80. John 19:26–27
81. Luke 23:42
82. Mark 15:39
83. From "I See the Crowd in Pilate's Hall" by Horatius Bonar, 1856.
84. Mathew 27:28–30
85. Matthew 27:39–42
86. Stott, *Cross of Christ*, 59–60.
87. Luke 23:34
88. Richard Allen Bodey, *Voice from the Cross: Classic Sermons on the Seven Last Words of Christ* (Grand Rapids, MI: Kregel, 2000), 57–58.
89. R. C. Sproul, Saved from What?, 84.
90. 1 Corinthians 15:20, 17 (NIV)
91. Romans 8:34
92. John 16:33; Acts 14:22; Romans 8:17; Philippians 1:29
93. Hebrews 13:5
94. Hebrews 7:25
95. Spurgeon, *Morning and Evening*, January 11, evening meditation.
96. Habakkuk 3:18

97. Thomas Watson, The Art of Divine Contentment: An Exposition of Philippians 4:11, This cross centered classic has been reprinted by Soli Deo Gloria Ministries (Orlando, FL.: 2001).

98. Galatians 2:20

99. Peter Jensen, "The Cross and Faith: The Good News of God's Wrath," Christianity Today, March 2004, 45.

100. Sinclair Ferguson, Grow in Grace (Carlisle, PA: Banner of Truth, 1989), 59.

101. I recommend The Gospel for Real Life and The Discipline of Grace by Jerry Bridges; The Cross of Christ by John Stott; Saved from What? by R. C. Sproul; The Passion of Jesus Christ by John Piper; and The Message of Salvation by Philip Ryken.

102. Bridges, Discipline of Grace, 58.

103. Spurgeon, Morning and Evening, January 14, evening meditation.

104. Psalm 100:2

105. See Deuteronomy 28:47–48.

106. Nehemiah 8:10; Philippians 4:4

107. Luke 10:17–20

108. Thomas R. Schreiner, The Law and Its Fulfillment: A Pauline Theology of Law (Grand Rapids, MI: Baker Books, 1993), 15.

109. Galatians 3:1

110. Romans 3:24, 26

111. William S. Plumer, The Grace of Christ (Odem Publications, 1853), 195.

112. Romans 3:20

113. Sinclair B. Ferguson, *Know Your Christian Life* (Downers Grove, IL: InterVarsity Press, 1981), 73.

114. Romans 8:1

115. Luke 7:36–50

116. 1 Timothy 1:15–16

117. William Law, as quoted in Gary Thomas, *Seeking the Face of God* (Nashville, TN: Thomas Nelson Publishers, 1994), 135.

118. 1 Timothy 1:16 (NIV)

119. John R. W. Stott, from *What Christ Thinks of the Church,* revised and illustrated edition, Milton Keynes (Word UK; Wheaton, IL: Harold Shaw, 1990). First published 1958 (UK) and 1959 (U.S.).

120. Psalm 119:11

121. John Newton, "In Evil Long I Took Delight," *Olney Hymns, Book 2: On Occasional Subjects* (London: W. Oliver, 1779).

122. 1 Timothy 1:13

123. Chamblin, *Paul and the Self,* n.p.

124. Jerry Bridges, *The Gospel for Real Life* (Colorado Springs, CO: Navpress, 2003).

125. D. A. Carson, *For the Love of God, Volume One* (Wheaton, IL: Crossway, 1998) and *Volume Two* (Wheaton, IL: Crossway, 1999).

126. John R. W. Stott, *The Cross of Christ* (Downers Grove, IL: InterVarsity Press, 1986), 68.

127. Jerry Bridges, *The Discipline of Grace* (Colorado Springs, CO: NavPress, 1994), 45.

128. Charles Spurgeon, *The Power of the Cross,* compiled and edited by Lance Wubbels (Lynwood, WA: Emerald Books, 1995).

129. Charles Spurgeon, *Morning and Evening* (Peabody, MA: Hendrickson Publishers, 1991), 8.

130. D. A. Carson, *The Cross and Christian Ministry: An Exposition of Passages from 1 Corinthians* (Grand Rapids, MI: Baker Books, 1993).

131. Carson, *Cross and Christian Ministry,* 52.

132. Luke 24:27

133. Graeme Goldsworthy, *According to Plan: The Unfolding Revelation of God in the Bible* (Downers Grove, IL: InterVarsity Press, 2002).

134. Jim Elliff, "The Glory of the Lamb" in *The Glory of Christ,* John Armstrong, general editor (Wheaton, IL: Crossway Books, 2002), 77–78.

135. Bridges, *Discipline of Grace,* 19.

136. Ephesians 4:32 (NIV)

137. Bridges, *Discipline of Grace,* 18.

More from C. J. Mahaney
Humility: True Greatness

God detests pride, and yet we cling to it. Here's how to
escape its grip, cultivate humility, and glorify God.

ISBN# 978-1-59052-326-1 • US $12.99